Winning Your Texas Injury Case Against Greedy Insurance Companies

A True David vs Goliath Struggle

Law Office of Don E. McClure, Jr., PLLC
8866 Gulf Freeway #440, Houston, TX 77017   (713) 904-1735
attorneymcclure.com   Soytuabogado.com

Copyright © 2019 by Don. E. McClure, Jr.

All rights reserved. This book or any portion thereof may not be reproduced or used in any manner whatsoever without the express written permission of the publisher except for the use of brief quotations in a book review.

Printed in the United States of America
First Printing, 2019

ISBN-13: 978-1-7336718-1-1
ISBN-10: 1-7336718-1-1

Law Office of Don E. McClure, Jr., PLLC
8866 Gulf Freeway #440
Houston, Texas 77017
www.attorneymcclure.com

To My Amazing Family and Friends

Thank you, Edith, for being a wonderful wife, cheerleader, confidant and, most importantly, a great mother to our children. Whatever success I may find derives from having such a supporting wife.

Thank you, Natalie, Nathan, and Bethany, for being fantastic kids. Every day I learn something new from you all about how to become a better person, father, husband, and lawyer.

Thank you to my past clients and to my future clients. This book would not be possible if you had not trusted me with your case. Such trust is highly valued, and I will be forever grateful.

TABLE OF CONTENTS

Why Do I Need This Book?	9
My "Why" - *About the Author*	11
This Book Is Not Legal Advice	14
First Steps: What to Do — And Not to Do — After an Accident	15
The 7 Deadly Mistakes That Can Ruin Your Auto Accident Claim	18
Chapter 1: The Accident	20
Client Story: The nightmare begins	20
What now? Do I really need a lawyer?	22
Five Signs You Need an Attorney	24
Chapter 2: The Insurance Adjuster	26
Client Story: The call to the insurance company	26
But the insurance adjuster is being nice to me; do I really need a lawyer?	28
Is My Car Accident Case One That the Attorney Will Accept?	31
Chapter 3: What about my car?	33
Client Story: The follow-up call from the adjuster	33
Property Damage 101	35

Quick Tips If Your Car Is A Total Loss	42
Chapter 4: Meeting The Lawyer	**44**
Client Story: Surprise and betrayal	44
How do I choose the right lawyer for me?	46
What Will an Attorney Do for Me?	**50**
Chapter 5: The Process	**54**
Client Story: Finding peace of mind	54
Medical Treatment and Attorneys' Fees	56
How Can Hiring an Attorney Mean More Money in My Pocket?	**58**
Chapter 6: The Negotiations	**60**
Client Story: I did my job, now it is up to the attorney	60
Requesting Payment From The Insurance Company	62
Social Media and Accident Claims Do Not Mix	**65**
Chapter 7: Filing A Lawsuit — When Settlement Is Not Possible	**67**
Client Story: I just wanted what was fair…was that too much to ask?	67
The Lawsuit Process: A Brief Outline	70
QUICK TIPS: How To Protect Yourself On Social Media	**79**
Chapter 8: Other Types Of Injury Cases	**80**
Commercial Vehicles	80

Motorcycle Accidents	84
Slip-And-Fall	92
Drunk and Distracted Driving	96
Wrongful Death	100
Refinery Accidents	105
Dog Bites	111

Chapter 9: All About Liens — 115
- Hospital Liens — 115
- Subrogation (Workers' Compensation) — 116
- Child Support — 116
- Medicare — 117
- ERISA — 117

Chapter 10: Common Insurance Company Tricks — 118
- 11 Ways Insurance Companies Try To Trick You

Tell Me More About Cases You May Not Accept — 123

Chapter 11: Common Insurance Coverage Issues — 125
- What "full coverage" actually means — 125
- Worst-Case Scenario: No Insurance Coverage — 127

Making a claim on your own insurance — 129

In Conclusion — 131

Testimonials — 132

VIP Membership Program — 137

WHY DO I NEED THIS BOOK?

If you are reading this book, chances are you are worried about the different problems that can arise after a serious accident injury. Whether the accident happened to you or to someone you love, the questions remain the same:

- How are we going to afford the medical bills?
- What happens if I can't get back to work?
- Will I ever be able to get rid of this pain?
- What do I say to the insurance company?
- How am I going to get to work and school now that my car is damaged?

Just like so many of the clients we have helped over the years, you are probably losing sleep and the stress is making the pain you are experiencing even worse.

That is why I wrote this book.

My approach is to educate, educate, educate. I want my clients to know exactly what they are facing and what decisions they will need to make in order to have the best possible resolution of their case. I want them to not only know what steps we are going to take to solve their legal problem, but also *why* we are taking those steps.

This approach is very different than most lawyers and even most professionals. The old-school way of thinking for lawyers was to keep all of our knowledge to ourselves – to keep you, the client, in the dark. Most attorneys continue to believe that this is the way to do business. I could not disagree more!

My clients are almost all Hispanic, and the vast majority of them are from Mexico. And from there, most of my clients come from Guanajuato, Mexico (which have the best welders I am told). And even though I am still working on speaking Spanish fluently, I do understand the culture, tradition and people. And I love them all.

Being a lawyer in today's world is very challenging; there's a lot of distrust of lawyers and disbelief toward anyone claiming an injury. Juries have been conditioned by the insurance companies to assume that most people who claim that they are injured are just out to take advantage of the system.

The insurance companies spend big money telling everyone who will listen that Tort Reform (laws that make it much more difficult for injured people to get justice) was needed. And while there are a small number of people out there making fraudulent claims, most people are making claims because they are truly hurt! A few bad apples have spoiled the bunch for those people who are sincerely injured.

Although this makes my job much tougher, I continue to slug it out with the insurance companies. The innocent and injured person just trying to get what is fair from the uncaring and greedy insurance companies has certainly become a modern-day David vs. Goliath situation.

MY WHY

I suggest that everyone examine their life to find their "Why" — whatever it is that motivates you and serves as a guiding principle for your life. Your "why" doesn't just fall into your lap, but is something that takes time and effort to discover. The journey is worth the investment. It is easy to point to our spouses and/or our children as our "why", but I believe that we must look deeper.

My journey to find my "why" began many years ago when I was playing soccer and it continues to evolve today. Back in the early 1990's, I played soccer with a largely Hispanic group of people and I was often the lone "gringo." We played in three leagues: one men's-only league in Missouri City, one co-ed league in Bush park (crazy drive), and one indoor league.

Over the years, this group became extremely close, and I have fond memories of visiting their homes to celebrate life itself. I became close to their spouses and to their children, and I admired their sense of family and community. And though I no longer play soccer, I can honestly say that those years were some of the best in my life.

During that time, I began to notice that my friends were sometimes taken advantage of by others because of a lack of English language skills or their immigration status — or sometimes just because they were Hispanic. Through my interactions with them, I found that I had a heart for immigrants and for the families of such immigrants. And while my Spanish language skills have never been the best, I was able to gain their trust as far as trying to help them through difficult times.

Who was to know that I would later marry a Mexican from Guanajuato, Mexico! Looking back, I now see clearly that I was born to be in a big, Hispanic family. And while it has been a huge cultural adjustment, both for me and for Edith, I am such a better person because of my new family. I really feel that I am a "reverse coconut", meaning that I am white on the outside, but brown on the inside. I am proud to say that my children are Mexican-Americans! I am also very happy to be so accepted into my wife's family and to be trusted by my many Hispanic clients.

My first meal with Edith and her mom was a soup known as "Pozole," which in this case had apparently been "upgraded" with pig's ear. I learned a big lesson that day — even though I could not speak Spanish with Edith's mom, as long as I smiled and ate her food, everything was good! No wonder we still get along so well to this day. Be sure to ask Edith for more details about how we met when you see her!

Edith is usually one of the first points of contact when you call or visit the office. She is honored to be trusted enough by our clients to be there not only in their bad times, but also during their good times. As Edith always says, she does not take that relationship and trust for granted. After all, we are family.

Since marrying Edith, 90% of my clients are Hispanic and 80% of those people are somehow connected to Edith's home State of Guanajuato, Mexico. They have become my family and I feel compelled to do everything I can to protect them from legal harm. Or at the least, to educate them so that they can make their best choices. I am so proud to be able to trace almost every one of my clients to another client I previously helped. And while I certainly believe in internet marketing, I am happiest when I receive a word-of-mouth referral. That means I am doing something right.

However, in the end, being a lawyer is just "what" I do, not "who" I am. I am a husband, a father, a baseball/soccer coach, a taxi driver for my kids, a cook, and a lawn care provider. Edith and I have three wonderful children and a strong relationship with God.

In other words, I am probably just like you.

THIS BOOK IS NOT LEGAL ADVICE

While we appreciate that you are taking the time to read this publication, we want to remind you that it should not be considered legal advice. The suggestions and recommendations in this book are purely for educational purposes only and an attorney-client privilege does not exist until we both enter into a written agreement outlining the terms of legal representation. We do, however, offer free legal consultations and would be happy to discuss your case in person or over the phone and give personalized legal advice once all of the facts of your potential case are understood. Simply call us at 713-904-1735 to schedule your appointment.

FIRST STEPS:
WHAT TO DO - AND NOT DO - AFTER AN ACCIDENT

The first step after any accident is to make sure that you and your passengers are not hurt in any manner. If you suspect that someone is injured or may be injured, call 911 immediately, even in a minor wreck.

Next, make sure that you and your car are in a safe location. Your safety is the number one consideration immediately following a wreck.

If it is safe to do so, talk to the other drivers of the vehicles involved in the collision. Get their names and contact information, as well as driver's license and insurance information. Write down everything from their driver's licenses, including the state of issue and their drivers' license number. Their insurance information is also critical, so make sure you note both the name of the insurance company as well as the policy number. The easiest way to collect all this information is to simply take a picture with your phone of any information such as the other person's drivers' license and the insurance card. If the driver of the car is not the owner, be sure to get the owner's contact information as well.

Do not make any statement to the other driver or their passengers with regard to fault.

Once the police arrive, make sure that you have all of the other person's information as well as the officer's name, the name of his police agency, and the accident case number. Take your own notes about the car crash and the location. Take photographs of all cars and of the scene. Scene pictures, pictures of the damage to the cars and how the cars came to rest after the wreck can make or break a case. Note any rubber marks on the pavement or other indicators of where the impact may have occurred. Notes and photos of the scene will help you recall details later. Write down information about all vehicles involved, including license plate number, year, make, model, and color, as well as any visible damage related to the accident.

Be sure to find any possible witnesses. Often, a person stops to check on the occupants of a car, and then the person leaves. If someone stops or if someone saw the wreck, be sure to get the name and contact information of that person.

Do I still need to make a police report for a property damage only accident?

The short answer is "yes"! If nobody was injured, if the damage was minimal and if the police are busy, they may decide not to investigate. However, I believe that you should always call the police and ask them to investigate the accident. I cannot tell you the number of times where one party admits fault at the scene and then they all agree not to call the police…only to have that responsible driver tell their insurance company that the innocent person was actually the one who caused the wreck. Don't do this to yourself.

If the police do not show up, at least gather the following information:
- Location of the accident
- Year, Make and Model for all vehicles involved

- Names, addresses, dates of birth and phone numbers of all drivers
- The VIN number or license plate number (take a picture)
- Driver's License information (take a picture if possible); and
- The name of the other person's insurance information as well as the policy number (again, take a picture of the insurance card if possible)

It is also important to gather:
- Photographs of both vehicles and any damage they have sustained
- Photographs of where the vehicles are located in comparison to each other on the road
- Photographs of any other landmarks that may have been affected in the wreck (telephone poles, other by-standing cars, etc.)
- Names, phone numbers, and statements of any witnesses who might have seen what happened
- Information on what the weather conditions were like at the time of the crash

Most importantly, do not assume responsibility for the accident. You can help those who are injured or need assistance, but even if you feel responsible for the accident, you could discover later that it actually was not your fault at all.

THE 7 DEADLY MISTAKES THAT CAN RUIN YOUR AUTO ACCIDENT CLAIM

1. Saying too much to the insurance adjuster
Regardless of how nice the adjuster sounds over the phone, the purpose of the recorded statement is to use your words against you later and pay you as little as possible.

2. Signing paperwork from the insurance company without an attorney's review
It is never a good idea to sign paperwork without first making sure that your best interests are protected. On more than one occasion have I met with a potential client who has unknowingly signed away all of his rights as to his injuries when all he thought he had signed was a release for the damages to his car. Don't be that person!

3. Not seeking the proper medical treatment soon after the accident
The more time that passes before you seek treatment, the more likely it is that the adjuster will find reason to believe that your injuries were caused by something other than the accident, ultimately refusing to pay for the treatment you'll need later.

4. Settling your case before your medical treatment is complete
Agreeing to what may seem like a reasonable amount now,

before you have had the chance to understand what medical treatment you will continue to need for your injuries, will spell nothing but problems later. This is a common insurance company tactic. Be aware.

5. Not documenting all aspects of your case
You must make sure that you have documentation to back up the requests for things like out-of-pocket co-pays, prescription costs, lost wages, compensation for pain you've endured since the accident, and travel expenses getting to and from medical treatments.

6. Not being honest with your attorney
Hiding embarrassing or seemingly meaningless information now will only become a bigger problem later on if your attorney doesn't have a chance to come up with a game plan for you on how to handle it.

7. Pretending your injuries are worse than they really are
Trying to get the insurance company to pay for problems that don't exist is a sure-fire way to land yourself in hot water. Don't exaggerate your injuries, be upfront about past injuries and claims and be honest about your pain levels.

DON'T MAKE THESE SAME MISTAKES!

Chapter 1: The Accident

Client Story – The nightmare begins

Happily ever-after. That is how the story always ends ... right? You work hard, attend your kids' school functions, socialize with family and friends, and try to be a good person. And in the end, aren't we all supposed to realize the American dream of true happiness and abundant wealth? Or at least enough to be proud of how hard you worked all of those years?

But something has happened and now you are merely trying to survive. After a few hours of work on a Saturday, you met up with some friends and family for a friendly game of soccer and to share a few laughs. Your daughter joins you because she likes kicking the soccer ball around her cousins. After a fun but semi-competitive game, you seatbelt your daughter into her booster chair and rush home to take a shower for a Quinceañera later that night.

As you are getting dressed, your wife realizes she forgot to get a birthday card for the party and asks you to run to the store. You get back into the car and head for the closest store, where you pick out the best card you can find for your "ahijad" (Goddaughter), smiling when you think about how excited she will be with the gift your family got for her. When you leave the store, you get stuck at a red light just around the corner from your home. Your light turns green and you begin to move forward ... well, that is all you really remember ...

Back home, your wife and kids are waiting. At first, your wife was upset that you were taking so long, but now she's worried. She heard sirens earlier and never gave it a second thought ... but now she's growing concerned. She hurriedly puts the kids in her car and drives toward the nearest store. And there she and the kids see what is left of your car. The driver's side has been smashed in, the side windows are shattered, and the airbags have deployed. The car had gone over the curb, where it came to rest.

The kids are crying as your wife pulls to the side. When the police officer realizes this is your wife and kids, he immediately tells your wife that there was a terrible accident, hands her a piece of paper and explains that you have been transported to the local hospital. And as your wife pulls forward, she sees a truck parked off to the side and notices its entire front end is caved in. All your wife can think about is getting to the hospital.

Your wife and children arrive at the emergency room, where she is told that she will have to wait to talk to the doctor. She has already called her Comadre and soon enough, the hospital lobby is full of worried family. Finally, a doctor comes out to say that you have suffered two broken ribs, a concussion, and that it will take some time to find out exactly what else could be wrong with you. The good news is that you are conscious and your wife is allowed into the hospital room. She sees you plugged into all sorts of machines, with an IV coming out of your wrist. She tries to act brave, but she bursts out in tears. She is just thankful that you are alive. And whatever tomorrow brings, she knows that together, you two can get through anything.

What Now: Do I really need a lawyer?

After being injured in an accident, most people first want to make sure they and their families are physically ok and *then* they worry about the damage to their car. At that moment, they are more focused on how to put the pieces of their lives back together rather than considering the long-term issues that can arise.

Many people are facing:
- Serious, debilitating injuries
- The inability to work and the fear of losing their jobs
- Mounting medical bills
- A damaged and often totaled car

The truth is, very few people *want* to hire a lawyer and they don't want to think about filing a lawsuit against somebody else (they don't realize that the insurance company typically pays for the damage, not the individual, and that lawsuits are rarely filed because most car wrecks are resolved through a claims process).

After all, they think, it was just an accident. And in the age of the internet, you might think that you can research and find all of the answers you will need to handle your own case. But, it is not that easy. Further, research has shown that people who hire an attorney to handle their personal injury claim receive a significantly better settlement than those who try to handle their injury claim on their own.

In 2004, the Insurance Research Council determined that people who were represented by an attorney received, on average, three-and-a-half times *more* money in settlement than those who handled the claim on their own. And that was AFTER the attorney was paid his/her fees. This determination came from an organization hired by the insurance companies — not by a plaintiff attorney's injury organization (see page 59 for details).

The bottom line is that you will do yourself a world of good by hiring the right attorney.

The other thing many people don't realize is that the insurance company's sole purpose is to make sure to settle the claim as cheaply as possible. This means that the insurance companies and their adjusters are motivated to give you as little money as possible for things like:
- Medical expenses
- Lost wages
- Pain and suffering
- Future medical costs

The insurance company will make everything difficult, from not answering phone calls to not approving services that you have a right to. For sure, dealing with an adjuster from an insurance company is a real hassle. That is also why it is important for you to have someone in your corner, protecting your legal rights against the insurance giants who settle claims as cheaply as possible.

FIVE SIGNS YOU NEED AN ATTORNEY

If the following statements apply to your situation after the accident, you may benefit from the help of an experienced lawyer:

1. The accident was not caused by you (you were struck by someone else or were the passenger in a car that was involved in an accident).

While not the ultimate determination of fault in a wreck, a ticket for causing a wreck will cause a diligent attorney concern about handling the case.

2. You sustained injuries as a result of the accident (this includes situations when the accident causes re-injury to old medical problems like past surgeries).

If your injuries were not serious, then you may not need a lawyer. For example, if your medical bill was only $1,000, then I would still advise you to give an attorney a call, but realize that the medical bills may not be high enough for an attorney to accept the case.

3. You sought medical treatment immediately following or soon after the accident
If you delayed treatment for months, an attorney will probably not be able to take care of your case. It is critical that

medical care is sought as soon as possible following a wreck or injury.

4. There is significant damage to at least one of the vehicles
This is a very subjective standard and people do get hurt even in what most people would consider a "minor" wreck. Pictures of both vehicles are critical because sometimes, one car shows minor damage while the other car is totaled.

5. The accident happened less than 18 months ago
When a potential client comes into the office with a potential case that happened several months prior to the meeting, it is a good sign that there is a problem with the case. In addition, because of the two-year Statute of Limitations in Texas, most lawyers are not going to get involved a case that is already close to the two-year deadline.

If all of the above statements are true, then you probably have a case that we would consider working. We are very selective about the cases that we take, as we only want the best possible results for our clients.

Chapter 2: The Insurance Adjuster

Client Story: The call to the insurance company
By the third day, you are finally discharged from the hospital and you are told to follow up with an orthopedic doctor to review the X-rays and MRIs. You are taking pretty strong pain medication and muscle relaxers. And when your wife, who hasn't left your side, helps you undress for a shower, both of you are shocked to see small cuts and bruises all over your body. You are finally ready to get some sleep, but the only way to find some relief from the pain is to sleep in an upright position on the recliner in your living room. All you really care about is being home and that your children and wife are nearby.

The next day, you start thinking about what to do next. Your boss already knows that you are hurt and will not be working for at least a few more days, and you worry whether you will lose your job as a contract welder even though you are one of the best in your company. Right now, you can't imagine picking anything up, much less welding the huge refinery pipes that make up most of your work. And you won't be crawling underneath a pipe or climbing the narrow stairways to reach a pipe anytime soon. Although you have some money set away, it won't be long before you will be facing a critical financial crunch if you can't work. And long term, if you don't get better, what will happen then? Welding is all that you know.

Your wife remembers the piece of paper that the officer handed her and she calls the insurance carrier phone number that the police officer wrote down. The insurance adjuster for the person who caused the wreck immediately seems to understand your wife's concerns about medical bills, what to do about getting the car fixed, and your inability to work. Your wife lets out an audible sigh of relief because she feels like she has someone to help her handle all of the uncertainty. She gives out a few details, but the adjuster insists on speaking with you directly, so your wife hands the phone over.

The adjuster expresses her sorrow for your situation and promises that her company will take care of everything as fairly and as quickly as possible. You're happy to hear this, but really you just want to get off of the phone — the medication makes you very sleepy and it's painful simply holding the phone up to your ear. The adjuster tells you that she is recording the conversation for customer service purposes and then asks about the facts of the accident as well as questions about your injuries.

The adjuster assures you that they are good neighbors and want to do the right thing. You answer her as best you can about the facts of the wreck ... that you were returning from a store, that you were at a full stop at a red light, that the light turned green and you started forward and ....that is all you remember about the wreck.

As for your injuries, you explain that both your neck and back are really hurting, that you have a couple of broken ribs, that you have had occasional back and neck pain in the past, and that you are just hoping to get better. The adjuster says that she will send someone to check out the car and to do an estimate over the next day or two. You feel much more at peace after this conversation and slowly go back to sleep.

But the Insurance Adjuster is Being Nice to Me; Do I Really Need a Lawyer?
Tricks the Insurance Companies Use to Get You to Settle

I have seen too many good, honest people get taken advantage of by the insurance company after an accident. One of the first ways that insurance companies try to get you to proceed without the help of a law firm is by acting like they are on your side. They train their adjusters to use tactics that will save the company money *if* the adjuster can get the injured claimant to fall for it.

Common insurance company tactics include:
- Having you give a recorded statement so they can use your words against you later. **Never give a statement about the auto accident to the insurance company representing the other driver.** If you are contacted by the other driver's insurance company, you are within your rights to refuse to speak with them. Be polite, but do not provide any information about the accident. Insurance claims adjusters are professional negotiators and will use any information you provide to hurt your claim.

- Presenting a settlement offer before you have had a chance to speak with an attorney. If you accept their settlement, you will not be able to pursue additional money for your injuries or for pain and suffering. **Do not sign any paperwork, including a settlement or a release of medical records, before you are aware of your rights under the law.** Lately, we have been seeing a trend whereby the insurance adjuster calls and gets a person to *verbally* accept a small amount of money to settle all injury claims. In cases where the adjuster calls within a day or two of the wreck (or even hours after a wreck), some people do not even know whether or not they have an injury that will need future treatment. These innocent people do not deal with car wreck situations very often and they are taken advantage of by the insurance adjusters who deal with car wreck situations on an everyday basis. Pure greed.

- Secretly checking your social media accounts to try to catch you participating in activities they can blame your injuries on.

- Hiring a private investigator to follow you around in order to prove that you are not injured.

- Telling you that they will cover the cost of your medical bills, then refusing to pay if you need more in-depth treatment.

- Coercing you into signing a medical authorization that gives them access to your entire, private medical history — not just the records related to your accident — to try to prove that the accident is not the cause of your pain, especially if you had old injuries or surgeries.

- Refusing to pay for the damage to your car by claiming that the accident could not have been the cause.

- Offering you what appears to be a decent settlement shortly after the accident and before you know what type of treatment you need — but failing to tell you that once you accept the money, your case is closed forever, even if you need surgery down the road.

- Dragging their feet and waiting an excessively long time to pay any of the bills, in hopes that you will get tired of paying for everything out-of-pocket and simply settle early.

- Counting on the fact that your medical treatment will not be covered by health insurance, leaving you with no alternative but to settle and be done with the case, rather than helping you find a doctor who will accept payment after your settlement arrives.

- One thing you must remember is that all insurance companies live by the motto "Delay, Defend, and Deny." Some march to this tune more than others (some insurance companies are notorious for being patently unfair with their low-ball offers and in those cases, we sometimes just go ahead and file suit).

- You must keep in mind that your case is just one of thousands and the longer the insurance company can stretch out the timeframe, the more money it makes. This is because the money that is owed to you is sitting and earning interest for them in a bank rather than being paid out to you. Further, they know that you probably do not have big pockets and that you will be slowly strangled financially, to the point of having to accept a terrible settlement.

Is My Car Wreck Case One the Attorney Will Accept?

I would like to point out some basic questions that I ask myself when deciding whether to take on a client's case.

The first question involves "liability", which simply means who was at fault. Is this a "he said/she said" type of case that involves a question of who ran the red light? If so, I know that I really need to look at the case facts and maybe visit the scene to get a better idea of who may be at fault. I do not want a case where a jury would probably find my client at fault.

I also ask myself if I can prove the case by a "Preponderance of the Evidence" standard, which simply means that more likely than not, the other person was responsible for causing the wreck. I must prove that the other person is at least 51% at fault for the wreck in order to move to the next question.

The second question involves "damages". If there is very little property damage to each car, then I really want to look at the injuries to see whether medical treatment is justified. There is no doubt that injuries are caused every day by what seem to be small wrecks, but I still have to try to convince a jury that the medical treatment was reasonable. Damages are mainly about actual injuries, but the amount of damage to your car can be important. Most insurance companies will not believe that you are injured if you have low property damage. This is contrary to what science and my experience have shown. Unfortunately, juries seem to believe that injuries are not likely in low impact cases. For that reason, the amount of actual damage to both cars does make a difference in the success of your case.

More important is your actual injury. Insurance companies want to see something visible like a cut, a broken bone or something easily identifiable as an injury. This is not the case in most car wreck cases. Most car wreck cases involve damage to tissue, ligaments and joints. What can be surprising to some is the fact that this type of injury can be more painful, can last longer, and is more difficult to overcome than a so-called visual injury.

You have a right to seek medical care and to even have diagnostic work performed. MRIs are a normal tool to get a proper diagnosis of your pain. MRIs and other diagnostic tools are critical in determining the reason for your pain and the insurance adjusters should not be allowed to dictate what is or is not proper medical.

If there is little to no medical treatment, there are not enough damages to make representing a person worthwhile. In that case, I usually explain that the Justice of the Peace Court may be an appropriate option for the prospective client. Again, we are very picky about the cases that we select as we only want the best possible results for our clients.

Chapter 3: What About my Car?

Client Story: Getting the car repaired
A couple more days pass and the adjuster calls to tell you that they have done an estimate of the cost or repairs for your car and emails you a list of "recommended" places to get it fixed. You look over the numbers, but you don't know what is fair and what isn't, and you really want to get your own estimate. The adjuster tells you that she will authorize a rental car, but only for the duration of the repairs, and that if you don't get started soon, they won't pay for the rental.

You do some research on the fair market value of your car and find that the insurance company's estimate of repairs is much less than its fair market value (what the car could have been sold for prior to the wreck), so you decide to get it repaired.

You decide to have the car towed to a dealership to have an estimate performed. The dealership finds several items that need to be fixed that were not in the insurance company's original estimate and you're now worried that the car, which is less than a year old, won't be able to be returned to the same condition as before the wreck.

Fortunately, the dealership deals with these types of details every day and they will continue to speak with the insurance company. They will even negotiate with the insurance company when it comes time to supplement any damage that is found after any work starts. This too is normal, as some broken items are hidden from discovery until the car is actually being repaired.

Meanwhile, your rental car is ready. It is about the smallest car you have ever driven and it will be tough to comfortably fit the entire family, but it is all the insurance company would approve. You hope the repairs will be done quickly and you can move past this point.

Property Damage 101

Initially, many people are more upset about not being able to use your car than about their injuries. We definitely understand the frustration, especially when it comes to taking care of the needs of your family.

But in order to best take care of others, you must take care of yourself, too — which is why it is *very important* to **not sign any release for car damage until an attorney reviews it** to make sure you are not accidentally signing off on the injury portion of the claim as well.

Can it be repaired or is it a total loss?
The amount of damage that was done to the car determines how your property damage claim is handled.

Let's take a look at the two types of situations you may be facing:

1. The damage to your car is repairable, or able to be fixed and the car can be made safe again.

2. The car is a total loss, meaning that the cost to repair the vehicle is more money than the car is worth.

Getting Your Car Repaired
If your car can be repaired, the insurance company will either have a claims adjuster look at it and give you an estimate on repairs, or they will ask you to get written estimates from different auto body shops.

Insurance companies will pay for repairs or replacement only up to a certain percentage of the car's actual cash value (usually around 70% to 80%). Actual cash value is the current cost to replace your car, minus depreciation.

Despite what the insurance adjuster tells you, **you are not required to use the list of "preferred" repair shops** they give you. The insurance companies often try to influence people to use a particular body shop. Since you have the right to go anywhere you choose, I always tell my clients to go to a dealership that sells the same type of car that they have and to get their own estimate there.

The company hired to do the repairs will most likely do a "supplement" where they will submit to the insurance company additional repairs that are needed after the start of the initial repairs. This is completely normal because in many situations, damage is hidden until the body shop opens the car.

It is important to remember, however, that depending on how your policy is written, the insurance company may not have to pay for brand new parts for your car – they could opt to cover only used ones.

Also keep in mind that you should be able to get a rental car that is paid for by the other people's insurance. Sometimes, you will need to rent it yourself and submit a claim for reimbursement later. If you do get the rental car for yourself, and before acceptance of fault, be aware that: 1) it is always possible in cases where fault (liability) is questioned that the claim could be denied and 2) make sure you get the cheapest rental car possible, as the insurance companies usually have a daily maximum that they will pay (and it is low). There are times when you may be able to get a car that is similar to your current car, but those times are few.

> **QUICK TIP:** *Do NOT give the body shop/mechanic the check for the repairs until the work has been completed to your satisfaction. This is critical, as this may be the only way you can ensure that your car is fixed properly. Make sure to thoroughly inspect the vehicle before you pay for such repairs.*

Navigating a Total Loss
It can be very frustrating to discover that the car is a total loss – especially in instances where the car was paid off or it had sentimental value that cannot be replaced. It will be the insurance company's goal to make this part of the process speed by as quickly as possible, so you won't have time to think about the decisions you are about to make.

Even though you are likely dealing with injuries from the accident, you will be tasked with finding a new car and accepting settlement on the damaged one. It can be daunting and stressful to find new transportation even when you are not injured, which is why we are happy to help our clients with their property damage issues in addition to their injury claims.

And Texas law assumes that you have the money to just go out and get another car with no problems. This means that as soon as the car is determined to be a total loss, the responsible driver's insurance policy will no longer pay for you to have a rental car. While there isn't a way to completely eliminate the stress of dealing with a wrecked car and being forced to "sell" it to the insurance company, there are very important steps you can take to ease a bit of the burden.

- **Know your car's worth.** The moment you think your car might be totaled, you need to start looking for a replacement vehicle while also figuring out the value of the car being totaled. Good places to start include Kelley Blue Book (www.kbb.com) or the National Automobile Dealers Association (www.nada.com). Also see our "What's my old car worth?" section below for more information.

- **Ask how the adjuster got to their number.** In most cases, if the dealer's estimated cost to repair the vehicle is more than 70-80% of what your car is worth, the insurance company will total your car and pay you its cash value instead of paying to repair it. And because insurance companies use a number of different sources to figure out what your car is worth when totaling it out, it is important to ask them which ones they used - being educated about the process could mean a higher offer.

- **Don't be afraid to negotiate.** Insisting that the insurance adjuster take into consideration the condition of your car, any optional or special features it has, or what it is worth to the local market could change what the insurance company offers. If you don't feel like you are getting a fair offer, don't be afraid to negotiate. Use written quotes for similar cars in your area and local newspaper classified ads to arm yourself with information. If you can prove that the car would have sold for more money in your area – especially if you live in a climate that is not harsh on cars – you might be able to increase the offer.

- **Opt to keep your car *and* receive money.** If you have an older car or have car mechanics in the family, it may be possible to negotiate with the adjuster to allow you to keep the car and collect money for its value, as long as you own the car outright. You'll typically receive what the adjuster offered, minus what is called the "salvage value." The salvage value is what the insurance company could sell it for salvage – typically 10% of the value of the car. Before making this type of arrangement with the insurance company, make sure to read up on salvage title requirements. In the state of Texas, if a vehicle was ever considered a total loss, the car must have a salvage title, but depending on the repairability of the vehicle, you may be able to apply for a rebuilt title. More information on salvage titles can be found here:

https://www.dmv.org/tx-texas/salvaged-vehicles.php

What's my old car worth?

To determine a car's value, you must figure out what a buyer would have been willing to spend on the car *before* it was involved in the accident. Unfortunately, the insurance adjuster is going to do whatever he can to save his company money, which means trying to give you as little as possible for your car; this can be especially tough when the car is older. It can help to have any receipts that show what work was recently done to the car, as can providing receipts for any after-market enhancements like stereos or special wheels.

As mentioned above, you can help prove your claim to a higher offer by using information about similar cars found on www.kbb.com, www.nada.com, or in local classified ads. Make sure to use both and to document your findings by printing them out or saving screenshots.

Make sure to have as much information as possible about the car including:
- Make
- Model
- Year
- Mileage
- Engine type
- Trim
- Optional features like sunroof, leather seats, back-up cameras, sound systems, etc.

You should be able to accurately describe the condition of the car *before the accident* as well. Many of the car value websites detail different values for a car being purchased at a dealership, by private seller, or at a trade-in. Figure out the fair market value of your vehicle under each scenario, though you will want to argue for a private sale value because that value is usually the highest of the three scenarios. Also remember that you are evaluating the car as if it was in the same exact shape as it was just a few minutes before the wreck – in other words, the condition the car was in before the damages caused by the wreck in question.

What paperwork will I need?
After you agree on a number for the fair market value of your car immediately before the wreck, the insurance adjuster will need to obtain your car title. If you own the car outright and do not make

payments to anyone, it should be a fairly straightforward process to send the adjuster the title.

If you are still making payments, the adjuster will have to deal with the lien holder (the bank). You or the adjuster will need to find out the payoff amount so that a check can be issued directly to that company. The remaining balance will be paid to you.

An odometer statement will also need to be signed, which allows you to disclose the mileage of the car upon transfer of ownership. Most insurance companies will also require you to sign a Power of Attorney to allow them to negotiate the title with the lien holder on your behalf. While Powers of Attorney involving property damage are typically cut and dry, make sure that the Power of Attorney clearly outlines what the document covers, so you don't inadvertently give the insurance company permission to make other decisions on your behalf. If you are still unsure about the paperwork that the adjuster is asking you to sign, feel free to call our office and we can take a look at it for free.

QUICK TIPS If Your Car Is A Total Loss

Total loss claims are a little different. In essence, a total loss situation puts you into a forced sale of your vehicle. Here are some helpful things to know:

- As soon as you suspect that your vehicle will be totaled, you need to start looking for a replacement vehicle and you should also be researching the value of your vehicle. This, of course, is very stressful.

- If the repair estimates are more than 70% - 80% of what your car is worth, the insurance company will likely total your car and pay you its actual cash value rather than pay to fix it. Insurance companies use various sources to determine the value of your car. If the company totals your car, ask the company what source it used to determine your car's value.

- The company might not have considered your car's condition, special features, or value on the local market when it calculated its settlement offer. Be prepared to negotiate with the company to get what you think is a fair deal. A company might raise its offer if you can show that your car would sell for a higher price in your area. Get written price quotes for a similar car from several used car dealers or look in the classified section of your local newspaper for used car prices.

- If you'd prefer to have your vehicle repaired instead of totaled, you can keep your car if you are willing to subtract its salvage value from the insurance settlement. Make sure the cost to repair the car will not exceed the car's actual cash value. To find out the salvage value, you can contact local salvage yards for estimates, but normally, the insurance company's itemized offer will indicate a reasonable value as to the salvage value of a vehicle (usually about 10% of the value of your vehicle).

- As far as a rental car, the insurance adjuster will cancel any rental once they determine that your car is a total loss. That is very unfair given the additional time that it will take you to buy a replacement vehicle, but it is the law.

Chapter 4: Meeting the Lawyer

Client Story: Surprise and betrayal

It has been four days since the wreck. The pain killers and the muscle relaxers are doing very little to help with the pain. You wake up incredibly stiff and it is hard to move. Your wife has had to take on your responsibilities as well as her own. There are muscle spasms in your neck and back and it seems no amount of rubbing, ice or heat helps to relieve the muscle tension. It is like your muscles have tightened into little balls all over your body. And your broken ribs make it difficult to even breathe. You just want to get back to work and be able to help out with the kids.

That afternoon, your compadre whose child had the Quinceañeras on the night of the wreck came by to check on you. They were so saddened about the wreck and felt torn about even going forward with their daughter's big day. Your compadre reminded you that there is a lawyer in his family who handles personal injury cases and has helped out many of his family members. The lawyer is a "gringo" but had married into the family through a cousin. Your compadre told you there was nothing to lose by making a phone call and that the lawyer understood the Hispanic culture and could be trusted.

While speaking with your compadre, you receive a call from the adjuster. Although they have agreed to fix your car, they are not accepting full responsibility for the wreck and for the injuries you sustained. You barely hear the adjuster's words because you cannot believe what they are saying. According to the adjuster, you pulled out too fast and you should have seen the other driver coming into the intersection. You try to argue,, but the adjuster points out that during your recorded statement, you admitted that you really didn't really remember how the wreck happened. No matter what you say, they are blaming you for 25% of the wreck. To make matters even worse, the adjuster says that because you admitted in your recorded statement that you had previous back and neck pain, the wreck didn't really cause your injury. So much for being in good hands!

Later that night, you discuss calling the lawyer with your wife. You explain that you are not one to sue another person and that you were just not sure of the process. Your wife points out that the extent of your injuries is unknown, that there is no health insurance to cover a lot of doctor bills, and then reminds you that the accident was not your fault. You both agree to call the lawyer the next day – to at least get some basic information about what to expect.

How Do I Choose The Right Lawyer for Me?

So, how do you choose the "right" lawyer? To most people, all attorneys look the same and sound the same:

"Tough"

"Aggressive"

"60 years of combined legal experience"

... these are some of the same old boring taglines. Don't choose a lawyer based on a persona you see in an ad.

I always encourage the client to apply the "El Paso" test. Houston to El Paso is a long drive (almost 13 hours and all in one state). To apply the test, ask yourself if this lawyer is someone you could see yourself driving such a distance together – alone in the car. If, when meeting with the lawyer, you don't feel comfortable after spending less than an hour together, don't even think about hiring them.

You need someone who really listens to you and what you have to say, who understands your situation and does not treat you just like every other case. Because even though the facts may be almost identical in some cases, no one is identical to you and your family. Hire someone you feel comfortable with asking questions and make sure that you like their staff as well.

Think about how you were treated on the phone and during the initial interview. And never feel pressured to hire someone. Personally, I know that I am not the attorney for every type of client.

I know who I work with the best and I pretty much turn down working with anyone that I suspect to be a problem client. For example, if the client seems to think that they just won the "lawsuit lottery," I know that is not the client for me.

Also try to determine whether personal injury is their main area of practice. I started out representing people in all sorts of cases and I can tell you that it is very difficult to be knowledgeable in so many different practice areas. So, as my practice matured, I decided to pursue only personal injury cases. There is so much law to know and I spend a lot of time learning to perfect my craft, taking classes and continually learning how to better myself both personally and professionally.

It can be challenging to figure out which attorney is best for you. As with most services, people tend to choose business based on recommendations from friends or family. But just because someone suggests that you call their lawyer, how do you know that the attorney will be a good fit for you and the problem that you need solved?

Regardless of the recommendations you have received, there are very important questions that you should ask before signing a contract with any law firm. Here are the top five questions that we at Attorney McClure feel are the most important:

1. How are your fees structured (How do I pay for the attorney)?
If you are injured and facing mounting medical bills, chances are it's going to be difficult for you to afford a retainer fee. Make sure that the lawyer works on a contingency fee basis (we do), meaning you won't owe an attorney fee unless the lawyer is able

to obtain a settlement for you. The attorney fee should come out of the overall settlement amount at the end of the case, eliminating the need for any out-of-pocket expenses on your end.

2. *Will I still be responsible for talking to the insurance adjusters? What do I do if they keep calling me?*
Make sure to ask the potential attorney what their process is for dealing with insurance company communication. A letter of representation should be sent on your behalf to the adjuster, notifying them that you are a client of the firm and that any correspondence needs to be directed to the lawyer and not to you. If the insurance company keeps calling you, the lawyer should instruct you to tell the insurance adjuster to call the firm, not your phone. You should be told by your lawyer to simply not answer the phone and that he will personally handle getting those calls to stop.

3. *How long will the process take?*
While answers can vary depending on the severity of your injuries and the medical treatment that you need, a good attorney should be able to outline for you general timelines and expectations. He should also be able to explain the full system for handling a case like yours, including help with figuring out the best medical treatment possible.

4. *What is your communication policy?*
Be wary of lawyers who tell you not to contact the firm directly and that they will only contact you instead. If something comes up in your case, you need to be able to reach your lawyer immediately. Look for firms that encourage open communication with both the staff *and* the attorney handling your case; it's always

positive when you are given direct access to the team of people working on your case. If you are getting the feeling that the lawyer is impatient or annoyed during his communication with you, take that as a warning that he will probably not be the best communicator if you decide to hire him.

5. How will you know how my medical treatment is going?

Also make sure that the lawyer is not afraid to openly communicate with your medical providers. In order to prove your case, it is important that your lawyer understands exactly what medical treatment you are receiving – as well as the treatment you are facing in the future - so having that channel of communication open can make a difference in the amount of settlement at the end of the case.

What Will an Attorney Do for Me?

Many people think that the legal process of handling a car accident care is fairly simple. After all, one person caused the wreck and they should pay the person who was not at fault. Seems easy, but it is not always that easy.

From start to finish, we easily have more than 50 steps we take to get a "simple" car wreck resolved — and those are all before a lawsuit is even filed. And while most cases are resolved without filing a lawsuit, insurance companies are becoming much bolder in denying claims or under-valuing claims.

For example, I recently heard of a case where the injured party suffered a serious brain injury after a wreck with an 18-wheeler. The insurance company was only offering a few thousand dollars above her medical bills. They offered nothing for pain and suffering, nothing for her lost wages and nothing for future medical needs (which were going to be necessary for her future health). In that situation, the injured person did not know what was fair and she took the offer.

And remember the job of the insurance adjuster is to be loyal to the insurance provider, not to the injured party. I sometimes wonder how these insurance adjusters sleep at night. Having an attorney to guide you through the process will bring you peace of mind and will protect your interests.

Besides giving you peace of mind knowing that you have someone who is solely looking out for your best interest and not their own (like an insurance company), enlisting the help of an attorney can take a huge weight off of your family's shoulders. A lawyer's job is to do the following:

1. Handle all correspondence and communication involving your injury with the insurance company so you no longer have to deal with their constant calls or confusing questions.

2. Help you find the right doctors who specialize in dealing with injuries related to car accidents and who are able to work with you even if they are not covered by your health insurance.

3. Investigate the entire situation, from accident reconstruction, witness statements, crash reports, and 911 calls, to ambulance run sheets, photographs, and visits to the scene of the injury.

4. Gather all medical bills and records to help prove your claim — even the ones that are difficult to obtain because of large healthcare facilities or difficult request procedures.

5. Analyze both your insurance policy and the policy(s) of the at-fault party to find all available coverage.

6. Work to find any additional coverages that may cover the expenses that the accident caused, including umbrella policies, policies belonging to others in the household, policies for the parent or guardian of the person at fault or for the client, or employer policies in the event you are struck by someone who was on the clock at the time of the wreck.

7. Make you aware of any liens (watch out for hospital liens, Medicare liens and even ERISA/health insurance types of liens) on the case to ensure the most money in your pocket instead of it going back to your health insurance company or to any other entity that helped pay for your medical bills.

8. Work with your healthcare providers to put together a comprehensive explanation of any future medical costs that you may encounter down the road, including the risk and cost of any future surgeries.

9. Identify the long-term economic effects that the accident has had on your life and your ability to earn income.

10. Obtain for your Lost Wage statements showing the toll that not being able to work has had on your family.

11. Put together a Demand for Settlement Package that concisely explains why the insurance company should compensate you and how the wreck has impacted your daily activities and life.

12. Ensure that the Demand for Settlement will cover all medical bills, pain and suffering, lost wages, and any future medical costs.

13. Negotiate with all of the different insurance companies to maximize your recovery, from all available sources of insurance coverage.

14. Negotiate down the costs of any medical bills, to increase the amount of money in your pocket.

15. File a lawsuit on your behalf if the insurance company refuses to offer a fair settlement.

16. Stay in touch with you even after the process is over to make sure that there are no loose ends that come up and to ensure that you continue to be pleased with the service that our office has provided.

Chapter 5: The Process

Client Story: Finding peace of mind

You and your wife meet with the attorney the next day. You were both pretty nervous – nobody ever wants to be in a situation where they need an attorney, but the uncertainty is just too much to bear when it comes to the future of your family. After a paralegal has taken down the basic information regarding the wreck, the attorney arrives. There is no rush and the attorney takes the time to listen to all of your concerns. The attorney takes the time to fully explain the process, and even though every case is unique, he gives a basic outline of what to expect.

Your immediate concerns include making sure that you get competent medical treatment and that your car is fully repaired. The attorney explains that while he and his staff are there to help guide you through the car repair process, the main concern for the lawyer is your medical treatment.

This is your main concern as well since you do not have any health insurance. And even if you did, you could not afford the co-pays. The lawyer explains that in these situations, some doctors work on what is called a "Letter of Protection". These doctors feel like they have an ethical responsibility to help people in your situation. The Letter of Protection basically states that, while you are always responsible for the payment of the doctor bills, the doctor agrees to wait until the case is resolved to receive payment.

The lawyer also reviews his contract and Power of Attorney. Ba-

sically, he gets paid a percentage of any money you collect. In essence, the attorney gets paid 33 1/3% of any monies collected without the filing of a lawsuit and he gets paid 40% of any monies collected after filing a lawsuit. In addition, the lawyer will be paid back any expenses he has paid out during the case. However, the attorney will receive no fee and will not be paid back for any expenses paid out in the situation where the attorney does not recover any money on your behalf. This puts all of the risk on the attorney.

You feel so much better after meeting with the attorney. The mountain is still before you, but at least you now know the path that must be taken. You also understand that while the attorney may be the "guide," you must still be the hero of your own story – for both yourself and for your family.

Medical Treatment

Every case is unique and different, but what follows is a basic outline of medical treatment in a standard injury case like in our story. It starts with you seeing a chiropractor for at least a few weeks of therapy. You might also see a medical doctor who may prescribe medication such as muscle relaxers and pain killers. All of your hospital records and bills will be ordered and reviewed.

If you are still having pain after about a month, you will probably get an MRI — although in your case, you may end up getting two MRIs because you have two main areas of pain: your neck and your back. If you do not have a herniation, you will probably do some more therapy and then close out your treatment. Hopefully, the therapy alone can control your pain. But if the MRIs indicate a herniation, you may be referred to a pain management doctor and/or an orthopedic (or neuro) surgeon for further evaluation.

A pain management doctor will evaluate you to see whether you are an "ESI" (Epidural Steroid Injection) candidate. An ESI is an injection into the epidural space of the spine that includes both a corticosteroid and a numbing agent. It is minimally invasive and can relieve pain in the neck, back, arms and legs that is caused by inflamed spinal nerves. Pain can be reduced for several days or even much longer.

Unfortunately, the ESI does not make the actual herniation smaller, but it does have the potential to significantly reduce pain. There may be some minor discomfort from the injection and it is always recommended that a second person should come along to drive the patient home. Normally, you will be re-evaluated after about 30 days to see how much the ESI helped to reduce your pain and whether it is still working to reduce such pain.

Once the ESI is done, you will probably have some additional therapy. If the ESI does not significantly reduce your pain, surgery may be an option. Unfortunately, most insurance policies only have a minimum of $30,000 of coverage to pay for towards your medical bills, lost wages and other damages - and surgeries cost several times more than that. The ESIs are already very expensive and, when combined with all of the medical treatment (including the hospital bills), you probably will have come pretty close to the standard Texas policy limits of $30,000. In such a case, a surgeon will draft an estimate of the costs of surgery.

In most cases, there will probably be no more medical treatment even if you still feel bad. It is unfortunate that the minimum policy limit by State law is so low. But in your case, after examining your policy, the attorney congratulates you for being smart enough to have both PIP (Personal Injury Protection) in the amount of $2,500 and an additional $30,000 in UnderInsured Motorist coverage. This immediately provides you with relief and reduces some of your stress.

How Can Hiring an Attorney Mean More Money in My Pocket?

The goal of every attorney who is serious about helping their client should be to get as much money as possible into the client's pocket as compensation for everything they had to go through, including time off of work, pain and suffering, and medical bills. But one common myth is that paying an attorney's fee at the end of the case will eat into what the client ends up with in their pocket.

A study conducted by the All-Industry Research Advisory Council titled, "Attorney Involvement in Auto Injury Claims" found that claims where the injured party hired an attorney ended up settling for more money that those that did not involve attorney representation. In fact, the study found that for every dollar of economic loss a person suffered, a person represented by an attorney received $1.59. For a person who did not opt to hire a lawyer, that number dropped to $1.26 for every dollar of economic loss.

Similarly, an Insurance Research Council study, "Paying for Auto Injuries: A Consumer Panel Survey of Auto Accident Victims," found that claims with an attorney paid out anywhere from **27% to 48% more** than claims without a lawyer (we are talking about more bottom dollar money in the pocket of the client -even after the attorney is paid). These stats in the chart below were compiled by the insurance companies – not by attorneys – and the numbers are eye-opening:

Type of Injury	With a Lawyer	Without	Difference
Neck Injury	$7,918	$2,480	$5,438
Broken Bone	$39,397	$19,105	$20,292
Lacerations	$4,771	$1,166	$3,605
Average Injury	$11,939	$3,262	$8,677

Once you factor in that attorneys typically help negotiate the medical bills and liens down, that still means more money in the client's pocket even after the attorney fee is paid.

Chapter 6: The Negotiations

Client Story: I did my job, now it is up to the attorney

The attorney made it clear from the beginning that your main job was to follow the recommendations of the doctors. And you followed those instructions perfectly. You didn't miss any appointments; you did your home exercise and you did everything the doctors asked you to do.

It hasn't been easy. It has taken commitment and time. At different points, you felt like giving up, but you couldn't do that to your family. They depended on you making a full recovery. After-all, you never want to go through anything like this in the future if you can avoid it. The therapy was, at times painful and laying down inside that tube during your MRIs filled you with anxiety. But you still moved forward. And when the doctor recommended an Epidural Steroid Injection to help lessen the nerve pain, you were just glad that you were not facing a surgery – at least not at this point.

Finally, you are getting back to being yourself. You are back to work, although you have to be careful about how you lift things. And at night, you continue to use the home workouts the doctors gave you so that you can continue to stay as healthy as possible.

You were glad to have both the Cervical and Lumbar MRIs so that you could know what happened to your back as a result of this wreck. Your neck had quite a large disc herniation and two of your fingers were experiencing numbness, but the ESI really helped to alleviate the nerve pain. However, you know that your pain could continue throughout your life. Yes, your pain has de-

creased, and your flexibility has increased, but it remains very likely that you will need future medical intervention at some point. You may even need a surgery in the future. It is the uncertainty that is the worst part.

Now, you simply wait to see what happens during the negotiations.

Requesting Payment from the Insurance Company

After all of the medical treatment is complete, a demand can finally be sent to the insurance company. A demand is a fairly short (2-3 pages) document that gives the basic facts such as the date and location of the wreck, who caused it, and an outline of the medical treatment along with a medical bill summary. At the end, depending on the situation, either a specific amount of money may be demanded, or else a "Stowers" demand may be made.

A Stowers Demand is simply a demand for the entire policy limits of the person whose negligence caused the wreck and your injuries. It is is appropriate when the injured person has incurred significant medical bills and/or may need significant medical care in the future.

For example, the minimum liability policy in Texas is a "30/60 policy," which means that, at a minimum, each Texas driver must have car insurance that pays up to $30,000 for one person or up to $60,000 if multiple people are presenting a claim.

If the medical bills total something less — say, $7,500 — a specific amount of money will be demanded that is less than the policy limits of $30,000. The initial demand typically starts off really high and the insurance company normally responds with a really low offer. For example, on a case with $7,500 in medical bills the attorney might send a demand for $24,750 to begin the negotiations. The insurance adjuster usually takes at least a month to review the file and make an offer. The counter-demands and the counter-offers will continue and then, you will get a call from the lawyer.

Ultimately, the decision to settle or not to settle comes from the person making the claim. The purpose of the attorney is to educate their client and to help them make the best possible decision given the facts of the case and the uncertainty of trial.

Contrast this to a situation where the medical bills are higher or where there may be significant future medical expenses. For example, in a case where the medical bills total $26,000, which is only $4,000 less than the standard liability policy for one person ($30,000), a Stowers Demand is made to the other people's insurance company requesting that it pay ALL of the policy to the claimant.

The Stowers Demand is a very powerful tool if used correctly because it gives the insurance company a deadline to respond with a fair offer. In the first example above, there was also a deadline to respond, but nothing bad happens if an insurance company drags its feet or makes a bad offer. In contrast, the Stowers Demand is time-sensitive and the insurance company has a lot to risk if they do not respond in a fair manner.

If the insurance adjuster is not reasonable, it is possible for the insurance company to be on the hook for a lot more than the minimum policy limits. This puts some teeth into the law, telling the adjuster that if they do not behave like a reasonable adjuster and pay the policy limits when it is clearly the right thing to do, then the insurance company could be responsible to pay out a lot more to the party making the claim.

Again, getting back to the example of a minimum Texas car insurance policy of $30,000, if:

- Liability is clear;
- The damages claimed are clearly going to be in excess of the policy limits;
- The deadline for the insurance company is reasonable; and
- There is an offer to take care of outstanding liens and claims for subrogation in exchange for the policy limits, then...

the insurance company could end up having to pay more than the $30,000 policy limits if they deny such a reasonable demand for the policy limits.

For example, if the insurance adjuster does not offer the policy limits in a situation as set out above, and if a jury comes back with an award of damages against the responsible insured that is more than the policy limits, then the insurance company for the responsible party may have to pay the jury award – even if the amount that is awarded is more than the $30,000 policy limit.

This is not automatic, and there must be an attempt to collect the excess judgment from the responsible party. In a normal case, the responsible party then assigns his claim of negligence against his own insurance company to the person making the original claim. This is because the insurance company has a duty to protect their insured and they were negligent in such duty to their insured because they did not pay out on a fair and properly presented claim.

The final piece of the puzzle involves the question of whether a person can send a Stowers letter to their own insurance company in a case where the responsible party had no insurance (or when they do not have enough insurance coverage due to the high medical bills). The answer is that a Stowers Demand only works in a third-party insurance situation and not a first-person insurance situation (where you are claiming on your own policy).

So, you cannot get more money than the policy limits of your own policy and you can only claim against your own policy in certain situations known as UnderInsured Claims or UnInsured Claims.

Finally, don't forget that until a lawsuit is filed, the insurance company does not have to disclose their policy limits. However, if the insurance company does accept the demand and offers the policy limits, they will send along proof of the policy limits.

> ### *Social Media and Accident Claims Do Not Mix*
>
> Sharing what is going on in your life on social media sites like Instagram and Facebook has become second nature to most. It is as common as picking up the phone to tell a loved one about your day.
>
> The insurance companies not only know this, but they also expect it and are just waiting for an injured person to make the mistake of talking about their accident online. If you were recently involved in an accident, chances are the at-fault party's insurance company will start monitoring your social media accounts.

Social Media and Accident Claims Do Not Mix, cont.

They will be looking for and analyzing all of your posts, especially ones about:

- Photos of the initial accident and how you explain how it happened
- Your opinions on any type of subject
- The language you use
- What you do in your spare time, especially if it involves any type of physical activity
- The places you check in and out of
- The people you talk about, especially those who may have been in the car with you
- Complaints you make

Why do insurance adjusters do this? Why do they care? For one reason:

Adjusters are looking for anything and everything to discredit you, claim you are not as hurt as you are, and show that you are not a victim at all, therefore they can get away with PAYING YOU AS LITTLE AS POSSIBLE.

Chapter 7: Filing a Lawsuit When Settlement Is Not Possible

Client Story: I just wanted what was fair...was that too much to ask?

Unfortunately, the insurance company simply refused to negotiate in good faith. The adjuster basically said that they did not believe that you even had an ESI performed! They don't believe the written doctor report and they think you are being less than truthful about the extent of your injuries. You are totally caught off-guard as all you really wanted was to be treated fairly.

The attorney explained the lawsuit process and your options regarding accepting the low-ball offer. You decide to file suit and to stand up for what is fair and just. The process is a slow and long process. You have to answer discovery and you have to give a deposition. You miss time from work and you worry about what will ultimately happen. Still, you know that you made the right choice. You realize that the case is not about suing another person, but about holding the insurance companies accountable.

After what seems like an eternity, you finally get your chance to attend mediation. Your attorney has explained that the vast majority of cases resolve during the mediation stage of a lawsuit. You understand that mediation is a chance to reach a resolution of your case without having a Judge or Jury make the ultimate decision about your case. You realize that at mediation, there is at least a certainty when it comes to the amount of settlement you are willing to accept.

And in the end, you are able to resolve your case. The road has been long and it has not been easy, but you are glad to put this matter behind you. Finally, you no longer have to worry about paying back the medical providers and you can move on with your life. You feel good about making the insurance company play fair, but you hope to never have to go through this process again.

About thirty (30) days after the mediation, the insurance adjuster sent over the final settlement check along with the final release. The attorney reviews the final release and you understand that you will never be able to get any more money from the responsible driver, nor from the insurance company. This is the final payment and you are releasing any and all claims that you may have against any responsible party.

The attorney shows you the Closing Statement, which is simply an accounting breakdown showing the settlement amount minus the costs, medical bills and attorneys' fees in your case. If a case is settled without the filing of a lawsuit, then the costs are usually fairly low. However, in your case, a lawsuit was filed. When a lawsuit is filed, the costs can go up dramatically and can include filing fees, expert witness fees (can be a huge expense), court-reporter fees and the costs for medical records, medical bills and affidavits. In some cases, you may see a reduction of the medical bills from the treating doctors. If there are any liens (see Chapter 9), such liens will need to be reduced through negotiations.

The check is made out to both you and the attorney. You will sign the back of the check and the attorney will hand you another check made out solely to you. In most cases, the attorney will also ask for feedback about what they did well and what they need to do better. And don't be surprised when the attorney asks you for a review! The attorney reminds you that he makes his living through referrals and that the best possible compliment you could give him is to recommend his law firm to a family member or a friend.

The Lawsuit Process – A Brief Outline

This is an extremely brief outline of the lawsuit process and is intended as an introduction; the entire process is very complex and each case is unique.

Sometimes, it is not possible to settle a claim without filing a lawsuit. This is most common with those insurance companies that only offer low-ball settlements. It is also a common occurrence when there is a dispute regarding who caused the wreck.

Lawsuits are also commonly filed when there is a dispute as to damages – specifically, what damages were caused by the wreck as well as how much of the medical treatment and resulting bills were reasonable and necessary due to the negligence of the person who caused the wreck.

The typical steps involved in a lawsuit include:
- The Petition
- The Answer
- Discovery
    - Disclosure
    - Interrogatories
    - Request for Production of Documents
    - Admissions
    - Depositions
- Mediation
- Trial
    - Voir Dire
    - Opening Statements
    - Plaintiff's Case

- Defendant's Case
- Closing Arguments
- Burden of Proof
- The Verdict

The Petition

A lawsuit is filed using a "Petition," which is simply a document that sets out the reason for the lawsuit. When the Petition is served on the person causing the injury (called a "Defendant"), the Defendant is then on notice of the claims of the Plaintiff (person who was injured).

A Defendant could be the person who caused the wreck, could be the owner of the car, could be the employer of the driver or some other type of entity or person depending on the situation. A Petition will set out very general facts to establish the proper court for the lawsuit as well as facts showing how the Defendant was negligent and how such negligence caused the injuries, medical treatment and medical bills of the Plaintiff.

A Lawsuit must be filed before the end of the "Statute of Limitations." Statute of limitations are deadlines that prevent a lawsuit after a certain amount of time has passed.

For example, say your car or motorcycle was damaged 5 years ago. If you decided to file a lawsuit now, Texas law would force your lawsuit to be dismissed and you could not collect any money from the responsible party. Why? Because in Texas, your period to claim damages due to a car wreck is limited to 2 years (the Statute of Limitations in Texas is generally 2 years for all types of personal injuries and damages from the date the injuries were caused).

This is a car wreck example, but other types of injuries may have a different period of time and there are exceptions in some limited situations. The purpose of having a Statute of Limitations is to encourage people to be diligent in pursuing any claim that they may have against another person or entity. This policy helps to make sure that evidence is not lost, memories are less likely to fade, and that witnesses are still available.

The Answer
In most cases, the Defendant will file an "Answer," which basically says that the Defendant denies causing the wreck and that they should not be held responsible for any injuries of the Plaintiff.

The Defendant, in most circumstances, must file an Answer with the Court before the Monday following the expiration of 20 days from when the Defendant was served with the Petition.

Occasionally, a Defendant fails to file a timely answer. In that situation, it may be possible for the Plaintiff to present its claim to the Court without the Defendant being present to fight the lawsuit. While it sounds like a great solution, when this happens, it is a pretty good sign that there is no insurance coverage or that there may be, eventually, some coverage issues. Also, the State of Texas does not favor taking what in this case would be a "Default Judgment," as the Courts want important decisions to be based on equal access to the Court and not just on what one party says happened.

Discovery

Each side will have the opportunity to conduct discovery. The most common discovery tools are Disclosures, Interrogatories, Requests for Production of Documents, Admissions and Depositions. The purpose is for each side to show the opposing party what they plan to introduce into evidence at trial. Discovery is also used to promote settlement before trial. Normally, a party has 30 days to respond to each type of discovery.

Disclosures

Disclosures are very limited and are scripted out by law. A party cannot "object" to answering these questions and they help to keep the lawyers from playing games with each other. If something is not answered fully, the party failing to disclose can easily put themselves into a very bad position – even to the point where their evidence could be excluded.

For example, each party must timely identify any expert witness that they intend to bring to Court to prove their case, and if they fail to timely designate, the Court could potentially exclude such a witness. The Disclosures also force each party to list any witness that may have relevant knowledge of any facts related to the case, whether the Defendant has been named properly, and even if there could be another responsible party.

Interrogatories

Interrogatories are basically questions that the lawyer writes up for the other party to answer. Objections are very common, and the value of the answers is sometimes very low, as the lawyers carefully word the responses. In most circumstances, each side is limited to 25 questions to each party. All responses must be sworn by the party answering the questions.

Request for Production of Documents

Requests for Production of Documents are requests for a party to produce certain documents or to allow inspection of such documents or other types of evidence within the control of the other party. Such documents could include phone bills, emails, recorded statements, and could even include inspection of a physical piece of property such as a ladder in a case where an injury was caused by a faulty ladder.

Admissions

Admissions are a less used tool, but they are a good discovery to use in certain circumstances. Basically, Admissions ask the other party to "admit" or "deny" facts that relate to the case. These questions should not be used to admit pure questions of law, but instead should be used only as to questions of fact. For example, "Admit or Deny that you ran the red light, causing the wreck in question" would be a question used to establish the existence of a fact. Sometimes, Admissions can help narrow down what facts are agreed and what facts remain disputed.

Depositions

Depositions are very similar to testifying in Court, but they are done at the offices of one of the lawyers. The witness is sworn in and everything they say could be used in

Court. There are many rules about how Depositions can be scheduled, who is subject to a deposition, the scope of questioning, objections to questioning and time limits. I believe that depositions, when well done, are truly the best discovery tool. You should plan on meeting with your lawyer prior to the deposition to be prepared by the attorney to give the best deposition possible. The general preparation will include advice such as telling the truth, listening carefully, never speculating or guessing, and to not get angry with the questions. Deposition questions can be invasive, and you may feel that they are not relevant to your injury, but the other party does have the right to ask most questions.

Mediation
Mediation is used as a tool to attempt to resolve the disputes between parties. Mediation resolves well over 90% of cases, so it is well worth the time and effort to attend — and in fact, most Courts will require the parties to attend mediation before they can proceed to trial.

Mediation usually happens at a neutral site and is conducted by a "Mediator." A mediator is a neutral party (meaning they don't have a stake in the outcome of the case). They don't have any allegiance to one particular party and all they care about is getting the parties to resolve their differences. An experienced mediator is usually a former trial attorney who knows the law and knows the Judges. A good mediator is creative at finding solutions and they are able to show each party their case weaknesses and their case strengths.

When you compare mediation to trial, mediation is a no-brainer in most cases. In trial, the outcome is always uncertain and by the time the lawyers object and fight over the evidence, the jury may not even learn about all of the facts they may need to make a good decision. At mediation, when you agree to a settlement, there is a certainty in the result. Yes, there will be compromise that must be made and there will be give-and-take, but at least you are in control regarding what you decide can be compromised. At trial, you lose that control.

The Trial Process

Voir Dire

Normally, a trial involving injury to a person and/or property is handled through a jury trial and not a trial by Judge. A jury is made up of people selected through a process known as "Voir Dire." Voir Dire is a fancy term which simply means that each juror is examined by the Judge and by the lawyers as to whether they would be a suitable juror for the trial at hand. Voir Dire is one of the most important functions of your lawyer and a good Voir Dire is critical in making sure that you have the best possible jury for your side of the case. Many lawyers say that Voir Dire is more about excluding certain people from the jury (people that would harm your case) versus selecting a jury. In county Court, 6 jurors will be selected and in District Court, 12 jurors will be selected.

Opening Statements

After Voir Dire, each attorney is allowed to make an Opening Statement to the jury. The purpose of the Opening Statement is for your attorney to provide a roadmap for the jury regarding your side of the case. Such statements are not considered evidence themselves and should be limited to discussing the evidence that is reasonably expected to be presented during trial. In a civil proceeding, such as a trial regarding negligence and the injuries that arose due to such negligence, the Plaintiff gives the first Opening Statement.

Plaintiff's Case
At this point, the Plaintiff will present his/her case. Witnesses will be called, which could include the parties themselves, eye-witnesses to the wreck, and expert witnesses such as the treating doctors. Documents will be filed as evidence in the case to prove the reasonable and necessary medical treatment (as well as the reasonable and necessary bills) received by the injured Plaintiff. The deposition testimony of a party can also be used by the lawyers.

Defendant's Case
The Defense is up next. They don't have to prove anything and they do not have to provide a single witness if they so choose that strategy. In most trials, the case really is not about who caused the wreck, but that could be an issue. Instead, the defense is usually more about attacking the medical treatment itself, trying to prove that such treatment was not needed and that the bills were not reasonable as far as the amount charged for such treatment. To attack such medical treatment and medical billing, the Defense might hire its own doctor to testify.

Closing Arguments

A Closing Argument is a passionate summation of the evidence and testimony that was heard by the jury. At this point, arguing the client's position is allowed. A good Closing Argument should emphasize the positive points of a case, while attacking the other party's legal position. The jury should know exactly why they should find in favor of your client and why the evidence should lead them to only that one conclusion. The most important factor in handling a successful Closing Argument, even more than pure talent alone, is for the jury to know, like and trust the lawyer on your side.

Burden of Proof

In civil cases in Texas, the jury must find that the Plaintiff proved his/her case by a "preponderance of the evidence." This simply means that a jury finds it more likely than not that the Defendant was more negligent than the Plaintiff. In other words, for a jury to find for the Plaintiff, they must find the Defendant 50% or more responsible for causing the Plaintiff's damages and injuries. And if the jury so finds, then at that point, the jury can look at the injuries involved and how to compensate the Plaintiff for the injuries caused by the Defendant's negligence.

The Verdict

The jury will go to another room and deliberate as to whether the Plaintiff has met their Burden of Proof. There are instructions to follow and they have a list of questions to answer. Once the questions are answered, they return to the courtroom to deliver the Verdict (decision).

QUICK TIPS: How to Protect Yourself on Social Media

To eliminate the chance that you accidentally say the wrong thing, the best thing to do after an accident is:
- Make all of your social media accounts private

- Do not accept friend requests or follow requests from anyone you do not know

- Do not post anything related to the accident online, including photos, status updates, or opinions.

- Do not post about your whereabouts, your workouts, your physical therapy treatments, or even reviews about the places you visit.

- Do not share opinions about others, including frustrations with insurance companies or those involved in or who caused the accident.

- Do not use foul language, discuss alcohol or drug use, or make derogatory comments about anything.

- Do not share off-color memes, articles, or jokes.

Taking the extra precaution now to be subtle and quiet online can make all the difference in your case and will most likely affect what you are offered at settlement time. Be smart and don't risk your case for a few likes or shares.

Chapter 8: Other Types of Injury Cases

Commercial Vehicles (18 Wheeler Wrecks)
It's not hard to imagine that semi-truck or other commercial vehicle accidents can cause serious harm or even fatalities when you consider that the trucks can weigh up to 20,000 pounds. This makes them up to three times harder to stop and much more difficult to control than your average car.

This also means that if you or a loved one is hit by a semi-truck, there are many more problems that you must deal with. Not only are the injuries likely to be worse but navigating the personal injury claim is extremely difficult since there are so many players involved.

As discussed earlier in this book, it is imperative that the injured person's medical needs come first. After that is under control, or a care plan is at least in place, it's time to look at who will be paying for the medical bills that will inevitably pile up, the lost wages that will incur, and the pain and suffering that comes with having life turned upside down.

To determine who is responsible for paying the claim, you must first figure out which insurance coverages are available. Various parties are involved in the truck's transportation, so you must determine the following at the time the accident occurred:

- The name of the driver

- The company the driver worked for

- The owner of the truck

- The owner of product that the truck was transporting

- Any other holding companies, leasing agents, rental parties involved

Determining the above will shed light on the various insurance companies that may be liable for paying the claim. Of course, all of the insurance companies will initially deny liability and try to point the finger at someone else and claim that a different insurance company should be responsible for footing the bill. But even if a company does not accept liability right away, it does not mean they are not supposed to pay.

If an accident involving a commercial vehicle occurs, chances are good the insurance company will be one of the following:

1. Hiscox Insurance
2. Progressive
3. Statefarm
4. HUB International
5. Reliance Partners
6. TruckWriters
7. National Interstate
8. Northland Insurance
9. AIG Truck Insurance Group
10. 1st Guard

The Federal Motor Carrier Safety Administration (FMCSA), the government entity that regulates commercial vehicles, mandates that vehicles be insured with minimum amounts to cover the cost of the accident caused by the driver.

- **$750,000** – Minimum policy limit for vehicles moving 10,001 pounds or more of non-hazardous materials

- **$1,000,000** – Minimum policy limit for vehicles hauling 10,001 pounds or more of oil, hazardous waste, or other potentially dangerous materials

- **$5,000,000** – Minimum policy limit for vehicles hauling 10,001 pounds or more of hazardous materials

- **$5,000,000** – Minimum policy limit for vehicles hauling 10,001 pounds or less of particularly hazardous waste or radioactive materials

These may seem like high limits, but if you are injured to the point where you can never walk again or you spend months in a coma, $750,000 can be eaten up very quickly by hospital bills. Not only is this one more reason why it is extremely important to have uninsured and underinsured motorist coverage, but it is also a good reason why it's important to figure out all of the available insurance policies that could cover the accident.

As part of that investigation, it is also imperative to find out the condition of the driver when he caused the accident. Many factors affect the liability, and discovering the following can make a huge difference in getting multiple insurance companies to pay the claim:

- What type of driver's license the driver held, along with whether it was in good standing.

- The number of hours the driver had been on the road and whether it was within the legal limits.

- Whether the driver had a criminal record

- Whether the driver was on the route outlined by the transportation company

- If the driver was under the influence of drugs, alcohol, or prescription medication

- His or her driving record, including number of accidents or traffic violations

- Employment status with the transportation company – was he an independent contractor? A temporary worker? An employee?

- Whether the cargo was within the federal weight limits

It can be daunting to figure out answers to all of these questions when you are also trying to deal with a serious injury. We have years of experience navigating these types of claims and can work on your behalf to figure out all of the people responsible so you can focus on recovery. Simply give us a call and we would be happy to help.

Motorcycle Accidents

Motorcycle accidents can have devastating consequences for both the rider and their families. According to the Texas Department of Transportation, there were 9,655 motorcycle fatalities and injuries in 2017 alone.

We have helped families with loved ones who have suffered serious, painful injuries as a result of a motorcycle accident and it is never an easy process to navigate, especially when there is a death involved.

Just as in car accidents, there are many different factors that contribute to motorcycle wrecks, but unfortunately the open nature of a two-wheeled vehicle means that the resulting injuries are much, much worse. Sadly, many times motorcycle accidents are caused by factors out of a biker's control, which makes them that much more devastating.

Some of the most common causes of motorcycle accidents include:

- Motorcyclists being struck by a car making a left-hand turn. Often a biker is proceeding straight through an intersection or legally trying to pass a car when the car driver turns left with no inclination that the biker is right beside them.

- Rear-end collisions. Distracted driving is worse than ever and is a major cause of rear-end accidents. Unfortunately, this is especially dangerous for those on a motorcycle because being struck while at a complete stop by a heavy car or truck can send bikers flying from the bike and into oncoming traffic, or cause them to smash into a vehicle in front of them, often resulting in serious injuries.

- Car doors being opened, blocking the path of an oncoming motorcyclist. This is especially common in areas where street parking is the norm. A driver parks their car, fails to look behind them before opening the car door, and then along comes a motorcyclist who doesn't have enough time to stop. The sudden impact almost always causes the biker to flip over the front of the motorcycle, causing injuries upon impact of landing in the road.

- Speeding. When cars are speeding, it is extremely difficult for them to stop suddenly, take curves in the road, or control their vehicle at a moment's notice. If a motorcycle enters traffic and a speeding driver cannot adapt, the result can be devastating for the biker.

- Dangerous road conditions. In heavy rain, roads become slicker, visibility is impaired, and stopping can be harder. Most drivers don't anticipate looking out for motorcyclists – especially in the rain – and accidents are common.

- Unsafe lane changes. Drivers who don't look twice before changing lanes are always at risk of striking a motorcyclist in the next lane. Many newer cars have lights on their side mirrors warning drivers of a car in their blind spots. Unfortunately, too many drivers become dependent on those lights instead of taking the time to look behind them. And because motorcycles are smaller than cars, there is a chance that the car sensor will not pick up on the biker, meaning the warning light may not trigger. If the driver does not fully check their blind spot, the motorcyclist will surely be knocked off their bike or pushed out of control.

- Driving under the influence. Whether it is a driver who strikes a motorcyclist while under the influence of drugs or alcohol or a biker who has had one too many and causes injuries to their passengers or other riders in the group, driving under the influence is not only against the law, but it can have deadly consequences.

What to Do if You Witness a Motorcycle Accident

Whether you are a fellow motorcyclist out on a group ride or are a witness to a motorcycle accident, there are deadly mistakes that can be made, even if you are simply trying to help. It is imperative that if you are attempting to assist a motorcycle accident victim, you follow these steps:

1. **Park your motorcycle or vehicle a distance from the accident and out of the middle of the road.** Even though it seems like a good idea to park closer to where the injured person is laying, it is important to park farther back for three reasons: first, parking away will give emergency responders room when they arrive; second, you will not be blocking the road, potentially causing another wreck; and third, you will give other drivers the indication that they must slow down and pass with care.

2. **Never try to move an injured person – even if they are in the path of traffic.** It is better to block the injured person with another car or flares than it is to drag them out of the way. Serious neck and spinal cord injuries can become even worse if a person is moved by anyone other than a trained professional.

3. **Call 911 right away.** In the chaotic scene of an accident, it can be easy to overlook calling 911. Don't depend on bystanders to do it; if more than one person calls 911, that is OK. Make the call, give them your location and any other info the dispatcher asks for, then do your best to write down or put in your phone your witness statement.

4. **Never attempt to remove an injured rider's helmet.** Even if the motorcyclist is coherent and asks for help removing his helmet, it must stay on. Even paramedics will leave the helmet on until they can get the rider to a trauma unit, since there could be extremely dangerous injuries or brain damage that must be assessed before figuring out the best way to remove the helmet.

5. **Only perform CPR or First Aid if you are trained.** You can accidentally do more damage to an injured rider if you don't know what you are doing, so don't assume that watching someone perform CPR on TV multiple times counts as knowing how to do it yourself.

6. **Take the time to get information on the rider or provide your statement to police.** Accidents happen so

quickly that any additional info you have on what happened will be greatly appreciated by a number of people. Writing out your statement or texting it to a family member along with your contact information can mean the difference between that person getting the medical treatment they need paid for or not getting anything at all.

Five Steps for Handling a Motorcycle Claim

Chances are, if you are injured in a motorcycle accident, your loved ones will be the ones caring for you, making sure you get the medical treatment you need, handling the correspondence with the insurance company, and dealing with all of the paperwork after the wreck.

We want all families to know that there are very important steps to take after a motorcycle accident to ensure that the injured person is not only getting the care that he needs, but also that he is not being taken advantage of during such a vulnerable time. It is imperative that after a motorcycle injury, the following must be done:

1. Photograph everything. Documenting with photos everything and anything having to do with the accident can make a huge difference in not only determining the liability of a case, but also demonstrating the severity of the injuries and the force at which the accident occurred. Make sure to take photos and video of:
- The accident scene
- The damage to the motorcycle
- Damage to the other vehicle(s)

- Damage to any landmarks that may have been impacted (damage to trees that may have been struck, bent poles, demolished landscape, skid marks in the road, etc.). These photos can help prove just how bad the accident was, especially if the injured rider was thrown from the bike or skidded across the ground. Any traffic signs, signals, or other important landmarks that could have an impact on the case. For example, if it is suspected that the person who caused the wreck was speeding, take photos of nearby speed limit signs. If they ignored a stop sign, take a photo of it. If the at-fault driver lost control going around a curve before they struck the rider, take a photo of said curve.
- Injuries sustained. Even if the person is in a cast and you can't see the actual injury underneath bandages, take photos of everything.
- The healing process, which helps show just how long it takes to recover from a motorcycle accident.
- Scarring as a result of the accident, including surgery incision scars
- The difficulty the injured party has trying to do all of mundane things that he used to be able to easily do before the accident. If your loved one can no longer walk up steps without assistance, take video for proof, including of the caregiver helping. Brushing teeth, eating a meal, getting in and out of a chair are all good examples of videos that can be taken for the insurance company to prove that the accident has had a major impact on your family's life.

2. Don't sign anything without first contacting a lawyer. This includes medical records authorizations, settlement offers, or paperwork discussing liability. The insurance company uses a laundry list of tricks to try to take advantage of injured people and signing something without being fully aware of the document's consequences can kill a claim.

3. Don't give a recorded statement. While we discussed the dangers of recorded statements earlier in the book, it is very important to remember that *no one* in your family should give a recorded statement without first having an attorney on the line with you. Insurance companies can easily fool caregivers or loved ones into telling them what happened – especially if the injured person is not in a position to speak over the phone – and the adjuster will most likely be very nice and convincing. Do not let them fool you and just politely decline any requests for a recorded statement; simply tell them that you need to speak with an attorney for your own protection.

4. Follow the doctor's orders and get the medical treatment you need. It can be tempting to want to get back to work and fight through the pain. Not only is that horrible for your overall health, but it also can give the insurance company the impression that you are not as hurt as you claim to be, which means that they will refuse to pay for any medical treatment you may need down the road. Listen to your body, listen to your doctor, and follow your treatment plan.

5. Consult with an experienced personal injury attorney early. Since the statute of limitations for a motorcycle accident claim in Texas is only two years, it is very important to get the opinion of a lawyer early on to eliminate the risk that you accidentally do something to ruin your chance of getting the compensation you deserve. We offer completely complementary and risk-free consultations, so you have nothing to lose and only helpful information to gain.

Premises Liability (Slip and Fall Cases)

A premise liability case is a type of personal injury case that can be a bit more complex than a straightforward car accident claim.

These types of cases occur when a person is injured while on someone else's property after the property owner fails to follow the duty of care not to injure that person. Under Texas law, anyone who owns property, whether it be a home or a business, and allows someone to enter their property, owes the visitor a duty of care to prevent injury or harm – even trespassers.

Common premise liability cases include:

- Slip and falls
- Elevator and escalator accidents
- Drownings or swimming pool accidents
- Exposure to toxic fumes or chemicals
- Burn injuries from a fire
- Injury by assault after failure to provide adequate building security
- Amusement park accidents
- Dog bites or attacks

While all premise liability cases involve different fact patterns and typical injuries, there are commonalities when it comes to visitors on the premises and their classifications.

All people on a property are considered visitors, apart from the owner. All visitors fit into one of three categories: invitees, licensees, or trespassers. Whether or not an injured person has a premise liability claim depends partly on which category their visit falls under. Let's take a look at all three.

Invitee - An invitee is a person who was given permission by the owner to enter the property for reasons that are of mutual benefit. Typically, an invitee is there to complete some sort of task or work; common invitees include:

- Employees
- Mailmen or delivery personnel
- Customers
- Utility workers
- Tenants

Licensee – In certain situations, a property owner will grant permission to a person who wants to be on the property for their own benefit or gain. This person is considered a licensee and typically include people like:

- Salespeople
- Social guests
- Household members or family of the property owner
- Off-duty employees (for example, visiting other employees, checking their schedules, or picking up their paychecks)
- Solicitors
- Police officers, firefighters, emergency personnel there to help someone

Trespassers – As the term indicates, a trespasser is someone who is trespassing on the property and does not have permission by the owner to be there. The trespasser is there for their own benefit and no one else's.

What duty does a property owner have to each type of visitor?

As we mentioned before, all property owners have a duty to prevent harm and injury to anyone entering their property, but there are varying levels of duty depending upon which type of visitor is there.

Duty to Invitees
Invitees are extended the highest duty of care and protection. However, if the invitee decides to venture off to certain parts of the property where he may not have been invited (for example, a customer goes into an owners-only storage area not near a common place on the property), he may not be covered should something happen.

Duty to Licensees
The duty to licensees is a bit different in that owners do have a duty to warn the visitor of any *known* dangerous conditions and to actively avoid serious, gross negligence, but the owner does *not* have a duty to inspect the property for the purpose of warning the licensee of any dangers the owner wasn't previously aware of.

Duty to Trespassers
It may seem odd that Texas law requires that owners have any type of duty at all to someone who is illegally trespassing on their property, but it is still the case. The only duty an owner has to a trespasser is to not intentionally cause harm to someone not invited on their property . Other than that, the owner has no duty to maintain his property in a safe manner for or warn a trespasser of any dangers on a property.

How does all of this factor in to my claim if I am injured on someone else's property?

It can be confusing trying to figure out where you fit when it comes to the type of visitor you are and the duty of care the property owner should have extended to you to prevent your injury.

Common questions that should be asked to determine who is responsible, or *liable*, for the accident include:

- Why were you on the property in the first place? For example, were you shopping at a grocery store or were you an off-duty employee there to speak with your boss?

- Was the accident preventable or foreseeable? For example, did you slip and fall on water right inside the entrance of the building on an extremely rainy day? Or did you slip on water that was seeping from a cooler in the freezer aisle?

- Did the owner make any effort to warn visitors of any existing problems or dangers? For example, were "Wet Floor" signs present? Did owner have an employee standing next to the water puddle to encourage visitors to walk around it? Did they have anyone actively working to clean up the spill?

The best way to figure out whether your injury falls under a Premise Liability claim against the property owner is to speak with our office. We can look at the facts, look at your injuries, compare them to the laws, and determine your best plan of action, all at no charge.

Drunk (and Distracted) Driving

Drunk Driving and Distracted Driving accidents are some of the most devastating accidents simply because they are 100% preventable. To make matters worse, accidents caused by drunk drivers are often fatal. It is not uncommon for the intoxicated person to walk away from the wreck with few injuries while an innocent life is taken.

According to the Texas Department of Transportation, a person is hurt or killed in a car crash involving alcohol every 20 minutes. Houston led the state with 89 fatal DUI crashes in 2016. And Distracted Driving is also at epidemic levels as texting and driving are common in today's environment.

The aftermath of either type of accident is horrible for everyone involved. The family of the deceased is devastated, the community mourns the senseless act, and the first responders must endure another tragic situation.

In addition to mourning, the survivors must navigate a complicated process of an injury or wrongful death accident claim which involves reports and insurance companies, investigations and medical bills. That is where enlisting the help of an attorney can help. Instead of having to figure out who to call and what paperwork to fill out, an attorney can take the burden off of the family and handle everything on their behalf.

The ultimate goal is to secure a settlement to compensate the injured person or their surviving family members for:

- Medical expenses

- Pain and suffering

- Lost wages

- Future loss of earnings

- Funeral expenses

- Grief counseling or therapy

Dram Shop Liability

Many times, the drunk driver's insurance policy is not nearly enough to cover the expense and devastation of the accident. That is why in addition to handling the claim, our office would work to find out additional information on the accident, including:

- Where the person became intoxicated

- Who else may be responsible for the accident

- Other insurance coverages that may be available

The reason for this is that Texas law allows for the bartender or establishment that *served* the alcohol to the intoxicated driver to hold some of the responsibility for the wreck if any of the following are true:

- Too much alcohol was served to the driver

- It was known that the driver was already intoxicated when they were served

- The driver was underage when they were served

Pursuing a legal claim against the establishment is called Dram Shop Liability and, if proven, can hold the company financially responsible for the injuries or death.

Social Host Liability

In certain circumstances, the "social host" rule could apply if someone under the age of 18 was served alcohol at a house party and then got behind the wheel and caused a wreck. Adults who were aware of the consumption of alcohol by minors at their home as well as older siblings who purchase alcohol for their younger brothers or sisters will often be held responsible.

Punitive Damages

Because drinking and driving has such permanent and devastating consequences, the state of Texas also allows for punitive damages to be recovered on behalf of the family who lost a loved one. Punitive damages are typically awarded when the behavior of the drunk driver before or after the accident was extreme, or they were grossly negligent in causing the accident. Meant to further punish the drunk driver for their actions, examples of circumstances contributing to punitive damage awards include:

- Excessively high blood alcohol levels
- Repeat drunk driving offenses
- Complete disregard for others by being especially reckless through speeding or driving the wrong way while intoxicated

- Lack of remorse after the accident

Evidence must be presented in order to prove a punitive damage claim and they require a stricter burden of proof, which is why it is important to have an attorney experienced with drunk driving claims handling the case. If you lost a loved one in a drunk driving accident or are dealing with serious injuries as a result of one, call us. We are happy to provide you with the support you need.

Wrongful Death

Losing a loved one can be devastating. Learning that they may have lost their life due to the negligence of someone else is even worse. Often, the family has to process the tragic loss while simultaneously trying to understand unknowns that cause so much pain.

Surviving loved ones are often left with questions like:
- How did this happen?
- Why did my loved one have to die?
- Could this have been prevented?
- Who is responsible?
- What do we do now?
- How do we investigate the circumstances surround their passing?
- How are we going to give our loved one the resting place and funeral they deserve?

Dealing with the loss of a loved one is hard enough when they pass for reasons the family can understand. Even when there are not questions surrounding the person's cause of death, you are most likely dealing with emotions like:

- Pain of losing the loved one
- Confusion at why they had to die
- Anger that you did not have more time to spend together
- Guilt that there was nothing you could do to prevent their passing
- Worry that you may not be able to afford the expense of a funeral, burial, and gravesite

But when it is suspected that wrongful death could be at play, the stress only escalates since the family is now tasked with figuring out how to navigate a potential claim. This means:

- Determining the actual cause of death with an autopsy

- Figuring out who is going to pay the medical bills that surround their passing

- Dealing with the insurance company regarding the person who caused your loved one to die

- Finding out who can bring a claim for wrongful death on behalf of your loved one

- Learning how to open an estate

- Discovering what type of survival damages are even possible

What does "wrongful death" mean?
Under Texas law, the definition of "wrongful death" is when the passing of a loved one was caused by a "wrongful act," carelessness, unskillfulness, neglect, or default on another person or corporation. It can be difficult to prove wrongful death without the help of a skilled attorney who has experience dealing with these types of matters.

In order to get the answers you need so that you can focus on celebrating your loved one's life and processing your grief in the healthiest way, it is helpful to understand how wrongful death claims work in Texas. This is no easy feat – especially during a time when you are overcome with loss and sorrow – which is why we are trying to break it down as easily as possible.

How long does a family have to file a wrongful death claim in Texas?
The Statute of Limitations for a wrongful death claim in Texas is two years. This means that the family is required to file a lawsuit against the responsible parties within 24 months of the loved one's passing.

We understand that getting to the point of emotional stability to even discuss a lawsuit can take time. Often, we are asked if it is too late to file a claim. While in some instances it is in fact too late to file, we are always empathetic in every situation and give families the opportunity to present to us the information they have to see if it is still possible to get a favorable outcome.

That being said, one of the best things a family can do after losing a loved one to questionable circumstances is to contact an attorney early and let them handle the hard parts so that the family won't have to worry or stress about approaching deadlines.

Why would I file a wrongful death claim in the first place?
When a loved one passes away, all anyone ever wants is to have that person back with them. No amount of money could ever make their death OK, especially if they lost their life in a tragic way. We are often asked how filing a wrongful death lawsuit will make the situation better. In all honesty, it won't make anything better. But it will make it a little less worse.

Wrongful death claims allow for the person responsible for the death to try to make right the mistakes that were made. The pain, suffering, mental anguish, and horror that your loved one had to go through before passing is devastating to think about. In a way, it is not unlike the feelings that the surviving family members are dealing with. Having the at-fault party pay to remedy that pain, along with the staggering costs associated with the death, is only right. The claim can pay for things like:

- Funeral costs
- Medical bills
- Burial costs
- Therapy for the survivors
- Financial stability that was lost when the loved one passed

Who can file a wrongful death claim?
Wrongful death claims can be filed only by certain family members of the person who passed (the decedent). Those family members include the decedent's:

- Surviving spouse
- Children
- Parents
- Adoptive parents

While the claims can be filed individually, some families opt to file together as a group. Siblings of the person who passed are not able to be included in wrongful death claims in the state of Texas.

We understand that the process can seem daunting and scary. That is why we are here to help. While we hope that you are not reading this because you lost a loved one to tragic circumstances, know that if you did, we are here for you every step of the way.

Refinery Accidents

In South-East Texas, refineries are as common today as cows and oil wells. They dot our landscape and you can easily see some of the refinery operations from the tall buildings of downtown Houston. And just as common, we see plant and oil refinery injuries. It is a dangerous business and work can turn serious at the drop of a hat.

But even though the jobs within such plants are dangerous by their very nature, employers still have a duty to make sure work conditions are as safe as possible. We have handled a number of cases involving serious injuries sustained at refineries and many of our clients have faced the prospects of needing surgery, especially on their necks and/or backs.

Common Refinery Injuries

There is a lot of money to be made in the gas and oil industry, which can explain why companies try to skirt safety in order to avoid slowing down production. This is extremely risky and time and time again we see workers suffering because of problems like:

> **Traumatic brain injuries** – explosions, falling equipment, or even being struck in the head by debris can all contribute to serious, debilitating traumatic brain injuries that can leave a worker in a coma or worse.

> **Fractures or crush injuries** – because refinery accidents are so serious in nature, it usually means that when a worker suffers broken bones, it is often so severe that sur-

gery is required. This is especially true with crush injuries; instead of a clean break that can heal with a cast, the bones must be stabilized with plates and screws, making the recovery time a lot longer.

Burns – as you can imagine, refinery fires are catastrophic. Even if a worker survives an explosion and resulting fire, the burns and permanent scarring can cause lifelong detriment.

Chemical exposure - formaldehyde, radon, hydrofluoric acid, and benzene are just a few of the hundreds of extremely toxic chemicals used in refineries. Exposure can lead to a number of neurological problems, permanent respiratory issues, or even cancer.

Hearing loss – repeated exposure to loud machinery or to the sheer volume of an explosion can cause a worker to partially or completely lose their hearing. In some instances, the hearing loss is irreversible.

Vision impairement – chemical exposure or being struck by debris in an explosion can injure the eyes in an instant. Permanent blindness is possible even when a worker is wearing protective eyewear.

Not all accidents are caused by explosions
Negligence is a common theme among refinery accident injuries; companies do whatever they can to produce the quickest results at the lowest cost and that often means overlooking important safety hazards.

As a result, serious injuries occur even in the absence of an explosion. Failure to maintain and inspect the working conditions leads to extremely dangerous situations involving:

>**Pressure vessels** – Cracks and damage can cause major leaks or ruptures, especially since pressurized units put out an extreme amount of force when something goes wrong.
>
>**Storage tank corrosion** – Over time, storage tanks can weaken if the metal corrodes the unit, the ventilation system is not working properly, or the tanks are not filled to safe levels. Aside from the risks of explosions or fire, any of these factors can lead to burn or poisoning risks if the liquid makes its way out of the tank.
>
>**Falling machinery or objects** – Hardhats can only do so much to protect a worker from falling debris or machinery and the longer a plant goes without proper inspection, the greater the risk for being struck by something overhead.
>
>**Deteriorating equipment** - Owners simply do not want to invest money into updating equipment and try to fly under the radar. Malfunctions of old machines can be deadly, no matter how safe the worker is when working on it.
>
>**Alarms** – All companies must have procedures in place to warn their workers if something goes wrong. But if the alarm meant to notify of a safety problem does not work,

the workers will not have enough time to safely evacuate an area.

Ventilation – Malfunctioning exhaust systems can lead to buildup of pressure and fumes that not only can seriously hurt a worker exposed to the chemicals, but also cause a major explosion or fire.

Lack of harness – if a worker slips and he was not provided with the proper safety gear, the result can be fatal. Even falls from a low height can have serious consequences if the worker strikes his head or neck.

Safety Procedures

While many refinery injuries stem from the usual culprits of an explosion or a fire, some injuries come from "the perfect storm" combination of mother nature and human error.

Refinery work can be risky due to the nature of the chemicals used as well as the actual processing used to make a product. In order to reduce the risk of an accident, it is critical that safety systems are not only formulated but also implemented. For example, there is a reason that most refineries do not allow workers to be present during bad weather. They call these "rain outs" and workers are generally told not to come to work or they are released from their shifts. There are also designated shelters for those occasions where there is not enough time to leave a facility when a storm approaches or when some other bad event is about to happen.

If almost every refinery around you calls for a "rain out" but your job still makes you come to work, that is great cause for concern. If it was foreseeable (meaning a normal person could tell that something was probably going to happen) that the bad weather was coming and that it was a bad idea to make your workers go out in such terrible weather, it is likely that the refinery was negligent in causing any injury. There are many other factors that can be involved in causing injuries, but the biggest cause is sheer greed.

Immediate Action Can Prevent Cover-Ups
Chances are that if you are seriously injured in a refinery accident, the company will do whatever it takes to cover up what happened to avoid taking responsibility. Enlisting the help of an attorney right after an accident happens can mean the difference between finding out the truth behind what happened and allowing the company to hide the accident's cause.

Attorneys can file temporary injunctions and restraining orders, which are court orders requiring that the company preserve the site of the accident and leave it as-is, preventing them from making repairs, destroying evidence, and covering up what really happened.

For example, in one of our cases, it appeared that a faulty valve released ethylene, which caused a flash fire in one of the process units. A Judge issued a Temporary Injunction to keep the company from tampering with the valve so that the valve could be properly inspected by all parties.

Refinery accident claims are complex and it's important that you have an attorney in your corner to protect your legal rights. We do this in a number of ways, including:

- Full investigations of what happened, using OSHA reports, depositions of witnesses and all parties involved

- Making sure you have access to the best medical care possible

- Enlisting experts in engineering, medicine, OSHA, and safety to strengthen the claim

- Ensuring you are compensated for medical care, physical pain, future medical costs, time off of work, mental anguish, and the toll the ordeal has taken on your life and the life of your family

We deal with refinery corporations' "profit over people" mentality every day. And as long as we have family and friends out there at the refineries – just trying to provide a good life for their families — we will be here fighting to make sure that they are protected from the selfish actions of profit-hungry corporations.

Dog Bites

Dog attacks are not only scary, they can start out of nowhere and leave a victim with severe injuries and horrendous scarring. The Centers for Disease Control (CDC) reports that dog bites account for 300,000 emergency room visits each year.

What can be even more frustrating is that often bites happen by dogs that the victim may already be familiar with, either in the neighborhood or from a relative's house. This can make it especially difficult to figure out how to get your medical bills paid for, since there are usually a lot of emotions involved for everyone.

Your ultimate goal should be to protect your health after an attack, allow for the best healing of the wound, and to minimize the scarring as much as possible. The best way to overcome all of these challenges is to understand what the laws are in Texas surrounding dog bite injuries.

The medical treatment surrounding a dog attack can be lengthy. Many dog bite victims face the need for:

- Ambulance transportation

- Emergency room visits

- Stitches or staples

- Wound care

- Infectious disease treatment

- Initial plastic surgery

- Therapy or mental health treatment to deal with trauma and fear

- Scar revision or scar removal surgery

Who will pay for my medical bills?
As you can imagine, the cost of these treatments can be extensive, especially if you are also dealing with the inability to work because of the attack. In order to receive compensation to pay for these expenses, a claim can be filed against the dog owner's insurance policy. There are three main types of insurance that may cover a dog bite:

- Homeowner's liability insurance

- Renter's liability insurance

- Dog liability insurance

The "One Bite" Law
In order to successfully bring a claim after a dog bite, a victim must get past Texas' One Bite law by proving:

- The dog's owner had prior knowledge that the dog had been someone else or acted aggressively before your attack

OR

- The dog owner was negligent in controlling the dog or preventing the bite from happening and that negligence resulting in your injuries

While it is not easy to prove, it is not entirely impossible with the right legal help. Enlisting an attorney who has extensive experience in personal injury and dog bites is one of the easiest ways to get past the burden of proof.

How can an attorney help me win by dog bite claim?

One of the most immediate things you'll notice about having an attorney help you is that you won't be burdened with intimidating phone calls from the insurance company. As we discuss throughout this book, there are many tricks and tactics that insurance adjusters use to try and get you to abandon the claim altogether. In our office, our clients never have to deal with the insurance company at all – we handle all correspondence so that you can focus on what matters most: getting back to health as quickly as possible.

Other ways that our clients benefit from having an attorney in their corner include:

- Finding all possible insurance coverage to pay for your injuries. Many times, there are strict exclusions written into the insurance policies that protect the insurance companies from having to pay for the aftermath of a dog bite claim. Not only can we identify those roadblocks, but we can find other ways to get past them.

- Investigation to get past the One Bite law. Even without blatant evidence like video, we can often prove that a dog owner knew that there was a risk of a bite or that they were being negligent.

- Maximizing your claim. An experienced attorney can clearly communicate to the insurance adjuster than your dog bite is not just a small incident like they want you to think that it is. Extensive medical treatment, time off of work, mental anguish, and pain and suffering are not to be taken lightly and our goal is to help the insurance company understand that and pay accordingly.

Chapter 9: All About Liens

Hospital liens, workers' compensation subrogation, child support liens, Medicare liens and ERISA — monsters than can gobble up your money

Hospital Liens

Texas Property Code Section 55.002(a) states that:

> *A hospital has a lien on a cause of action or claim of an individual who receives hospital services for injuries caused by an accident that is attributed to the negligence of another person. For the lien to attach, the individual must be admitted to a hospital not later than 72 hours after the accident.*

This lien is automatically granted to such qualifying hospitals and it "attaches" to any monies you receive because of the injuries caused by the negligence of another and for which you sought such medical treatment. In simple terms, this means that when it comes time for you to receive your check, you may have no choice but to pay the hospital their outstanding bill.

There are exceptions that most people would never know about, such as no attachment to workers' compensation funds and no attachment to first party insurance coverages such as Uninsured Motorist/Underinsured Motorist claims. That is a good reason to have an attorney handling your car wreck injury claim, as these bills can add up to a lot of money.

The hospitals are also required to "perfect" their lien, which simply means they filed a Notice of Lien in the County Clerk records of the county where the injuries were treated. If the settlement monies are paid out and the properly filed liens are not paid, the hospital could bring a lawsuit against not only the injured person, but also the attorney handling your claim. Finally, keep in mind that a good lawyer should seek to get a reduction from the hospitals so that you end up with more money in your pocket.

Subrogation – Think Workers' Compensation Claims

In Chapter 417 of the Texas Labor Code, you can find the law that gives a "subrogation" right to the workers' compensation carrier against your settlement. Any employee who receives workers' compensation benefits and receives money in a settlement will have to pay back to the workers' compensation carrier what they paid out on their behalf. The amount owed by the employee from a third-party settlement will often be reduced by at least one-third and, sometimes, much more.

Child Support Liens

Pursuant to The Texas Family Code, Sections 157.311 through 157.331, a child support lien attaches to any settlement for personal injuries. We recently went through this situation and it can be very difficult to get the Texas Attorney General's Office to take less than the total owed – but it is possible in some cases. And when I mean that it is difficult to get them to reduce the total amount of what is owed, I am only talking about reducing the amount that needs to be paid before getting any settlement funds. I am not talking about getting the total amount owed reduced.

There are many requirements as to what constitutes an effective child support lien. The lien only attaches to the net amount that is owed to the client once the attorneys' fees, costs and medical bills have been paid. In the end, you will end up paying all or a significant portion of any unpaid child support and that money will come out of your portion of the settlement.

Medicare Liens
If you received any Medicare benefits due to care for an injury you sustained in a wreck/incident and you collect money from the negligent person who caused your injury, Medicare has what is known as a "super lien." Medicare tries not to pay any medical bills that should be covered by an employee's workers' compensation plan or that should be covered by a negligent party's insurance policy, but sometimes it does end up making such payments. As a result, such amounts must be paid back from settlement funds.

ERISA
ERISA is truly a beast of a lien. ERISA is extremely complex and is covered by Federal law, which trumps State law. Unlike the other liens and subrogation interests listed above, they don't have to play nice and they do not have to reduce their bills.

Known as ERISA, the full name is The Employment Income Security Act of 1974 and it covers employer-based health plans (and pensions). There was a case known as the McCutchen case that has been interpreted by the companies providing employer-based health plans as meaning ERISA liens must be paid back 100%, even taking precedent over attorneys' fees, costs and other medical bills. As a result, there has been an entire industry built around collecting and defending such collections. Just know that this area of the law is very complex and continues to evolve.

Chapter 10: Common Insurance Company Tricks

Remember, insurance companies want to protect their bottom line, and many of them will try to do so by using a variety of ways to try to trick you into taking low-ball offers or accepting false information about lack of coverage. Here are some schemes to be aware of:

#1. The bait and switch. First, the insurance company will tell you that your medical bills will be covered and to go ahead and get medical treatment. You move forward with all of your doctors' appointments, go on to physical therapy, get the surgery your physicians recommend, then go through more physical therapy — only to be told by the insurance company that they are only going to be paying a small portion of the bills. This happens all the time and many people get suckered into believing that they really don't have a choice but to accept a fraction of a settlement they were expecting. Too much time has passed to hire a lawyer, the medical bills still aren't paid, and the person now feels stuck between a rock and a hard spot, forcing them to settle.

#2. The insurance adjuster gives you a deadline to settle, even though it is nowhere near the Statute of Limitations. Under Texas law, you have two years from the date of the accident to file a claim or a lawsuit, which also includes accepting a settlement from the insurance company. Having an insurance adjuster tell you that you must take or leave their settlement offer weeks after the accident is wrong and dangerous, especially if you are facing the need for additional medical treatment down the road.

#3. The adjuster is extremely kind and sounds worried about

your condition. This is a tactic to get you to trust him. He may say things like, "I'm so sorry to hear what you are going through," or "I am going to do everything in my power to make this right," or "Don't worry, we are going to get everything squared away as quickly as possible." It is easy to appreciate what seems like a genuine tone of voice and a genuine desire to help ... but take it with a grain of salt. At the end of the day, that adjuster's sole job is to save his company as much money as possible, which means giving you as little as possible.

#4. Questioning the severity of your injuries. The adjuster will use every excuse to make it seem like your injuries aren't *that bad.* They may try to downplay the property damage, question how you determine your pain levels, explain that they see a lot of accidents and that the pain shouldn't really be as bad as you think it feels, or perhaps even outright accuse you of not telling the truth. You know your body better than anyone. If you are in pain, it is OK to say you are in pain, and two of the best ways to back that up are to make sure your doctor is aware of your pain and to regularly journal how you feel.

#5. Attempt to claim that the injuries can't be from the accident at all. The adjuster may try to blame the injuries on your age, physical exertion from your job, sports you play or have played in the past, surgeries you have had during your lifetime, roughhousing with your kids, extra-curricular activities you may enjoy like skiing or rock climbing, or any number of reasons.

#6. Make you sign a medical authorization to release medical records not related to the accident. The adjuster will make it sound like signing their authorization is just a simple, routine step to getting your bills paid by saying something like, "My company just needs permission to get the medical records and bills associated with the accident so we can submit them for settlement, so just give it a quick signature and send it right back." In reality, the company will most likely comb through *all* of your records, searching for things to undermine your credibility (drugs or alcohol use) or to find other explanations for your injuries (previous surgeries, preexisting conditions, or past injuries). Don't open yourself up to those vulnerabilities; consult with a lawyer before signing *anything*.

#7. Making a recorded statement mandatory for moving forward with your case. Despite what the third-party insurance adjuster tells you, you are absolutely under no obligation to give them a recorded statement before speaking with an attorney. The recorded statement will be used against you later, no matter how innocent the questions seem. This is especially true if the seemingly-friendly adjuster tells you that it is OK to answer, "I don't know" if you want to. That "I don't know" will turn into the adjuster saying months later, "Then he didn't even know the answer to a simple question like, 'Who ran the red light?' He must be lying!"

#8. They will try to convince you there isn't much insurance coverage. Insurance adjusters are banking on you not asking a lot of questions and that you will take their word for it. So if an adjuster tells you that there is only "a little" coverage as an explanation why his offer is so low, chances are he is hoping you're not going to ask for the exact policy limit amounts. The adjuster also may not disclose the fact that there are additional policies which do actually have a lot of coverage, like an umbrella policy that is often worth millions.

#9. Offer you a quick settlement to "help you out" since money is tight due to your inability to work. If you can't make it to your job because of your injuries, the adjuster might use that as a trick to get you to accept a few thousand dollars to help you out and make ends meet. In reality, you are probably facing quite a few medical bills and the moment you accept a settlement, you are waiving your right to getting those bills paid in the future, all for the sake of a quick buck.

#10. Dragging their feet and taking their time moving the case along to frustrate you. Not returning your phone calls, taking forever to review the paperwork, or simply taking their sweet time are all ways that insurance adjusters try to get under your skin, so you are more likely to accept their low-ball settlement offer and get the entire thing over with. Or they will draw things out, hoping to get you closer and closer to the two-year Statute of Limitations, which is when your options really start to run out. When you work with an experienced personal injury attorney, not only do they handle all of communication with the insurance company for you, but they also do everything they can to move the case along at a reasonable pace. The insurance company typically goes along with it since they know they can't pull one over on a lawyer who already knows all of the insurance company tactics.

#11. The insurance company will flat-out deny liability. This is especially common when neither driver was cited, if there were witnesses disputing what happened, or if both parties were cited (for example, you were cited for not wearing a seatbelt, but the other driver caused the wreck by running a red light). The first step to trying to pull one over on you is for the insurance adjuster to simply tell you that they are denying the claim and that there is nothing he can do for you. So many innocent people believe the insurance company and don't question it, so it's a very common trick they play.

Tell Me More About Cases You May Not Accept

While we wish that we could help everyone who calls our office, many times it does not make financial sense for the injured party to hire an attorney when they can handle the matter themselves. That is why we do not accept cases where:

- The injuries resulted in less than $2,000 of medical bills. Not only can these cases typically be settled with the insurance company directly, but we wouldn't feel comfortable taking a fee on such a small case, leaving the client with virtually nothing in their pocket.

- The property damage is minimal. As hurt as you may feel after an accident, if there is little to no damage to either of the vehicles, it is going to be very difficult to prove to the insurance company that the injuries are a result of the wreck.

- You were cited for the accident. It is nearly impossible to dispute a police officer's citation, especially if you were the only one ticketed for the accident, which means that the insurance company will be adamant about denying the claim if you were deemed at fault and their insured was not.

- The Statute of Limitations is closely approaching. In the State of Texas, injured parties have up to two years to bring a claim by filing a lawsuit. Some claims are better settled out of court and not filed with the courts, but starting the settlement process too close to deadline is not only a nightmare, but it could end up getting you nowhere.

- You were already represented by another attorney who performed a lot of work on the case. It is one thing to sign up with an attorney, have buyer's remorse, and call us the next day for help. It is another to have the attorney spend months of time, effort, and energy on the case and then decide that you are not pleased with the projected outcome and try to hire a new lawyer. Not only will you get stuck with a bill from the old attorney, it will be difficult for us to simply pick up where they left off.

- Your injuries could be the result of serious pre-existing conditions. While we understand that new accidents can aggravate old injuries, if you have had multiple surgeries and are now dealing with pain in the same place after an accident, it will be hard to prove to a jury that your pain was caused exclusively from the wreck and not the previous operations.

Chapter 11: Common Insurance Coverage Issues

If I Have "Full Coverage" Insurance, Why Won't the Insurance Company Pay Me?

Liability, UnderInsured Motorist (UIM), Uninsured Motorist (UM) and Personal Injury Protection (PIP) Insurance Coverages

A common misconception is that "full coverage" insurance means that your policy includes all possible coverages that an insurance company offers. Often, "full coverage" simply means that your policy has the minimum of what is required by the state of Texas.

All drivers are required to carry **bodily injury liability insurance** with a minimum coverage amount of **$30,000 per person** and **$60,000 per accident** to help pay for injuries and **$25,000 per incident** for **property damages** if you cause a car accident. It is often referred to as 30/60/25 coverage.

But what happens if you are seriously hurt in an accident caused by someone else and they have little or no insurance? Unless you have Uninsured/Underinsured motorist (UM/UIM) coverage, you may be out of luck.

Uninsured/Underinsured Motorist (UM/UIM) Coverage pays your expenses from an accident caused by an uninsured motorist, a motorist who did not have enough insurance, or a hit-and-run driver. It also pays for personal property that was damaged in your car.

There is a mandatory $250 deductible for property damage. This means you must pay the first $250 of the expenses yourself before the insurance company will pay.

There are two types of UM/UIM coverage:
- Bodily injury UM/UIM pays for medical bills, lost wages, pain and suffering, disfigurement, and permanent or partial disability. There is not a deductible with this type.
- Property damage UM/UIM pays for auto repairs, a rental car, and damage to items in your car.

Uninsured/Underinsured Motorist (UM/UIM) Coverage will cover you, your family members, passengers in your car, and others driving your car with your permission.

*Insurance companies must offer UM/UIM coverage. If you don't want it, you must reject it in writing.

UM/UIM coverage kicks in when the person who caused the accident has too little or no insurance at all to cover your injuries, your lost wages, future medical bills, and pain and suffering. Accidents are extremely expensive, and even an ambulance ride and emergency room stay alone can cost well over the minimum policy limits. If you have UM/UIM coverage, you won't have to worry about having enough money to cover those costs because your insurance company will pick up what the at-fault company did not.

Every policy is different, but we recommend that everyone have *at least* $100,000 per person and $300,000 per accident in coverage. The cost is very minimal — less than $10 per month in most cases — and our office offers policy reviews completely free of charge. Simply call us at 713-904-1765 to set up a quick, 15-min review of the policy. All we need is your declarations page and we'll be able to make suggestions on how to protect your family.

It is also very important to have Personal Injury Protection (PIP) coverage. PIP is considered a "no fault" type of coverage that will cover your medical bills and lost wages up to the amount of the policy no matter who caused the wreck. The typical PIP policy amount is $2,500, but it could be much higher. Do not confuse PIP with Medical Payments coverage because under Medical Payments coverage, the insurance carrier will be entitled to be paid back for any money they paid out on your behalf once you settle with the person who caused the wreck. Under PIP, you never have to pay back the insurance carrier.

Texas law actually requires an insurance company to offer both PIP and UIM/UM coverage. You can reject it (in writing), but don't reject these coverages as they may save you when you are facing a situation where the other person had no car insurance or where your medical bills easily exceed the low State of Texas minimal policy limits of $30,000. Please call your insurance agent right now if you do not have these coverages under your current policy.

The Worst-Case Scenario – No Insurance Coverage at All

This is not a topic that can be fully covered in this book, but you could always sue them (Justice of the Peace Court will accept cases with damages up to $10,000) and hope to get paid. I mention Justice of the Peace Courts only because they are Courts designed more for the people and less for attorneys, but if your damages exceed $10,000, you will need to file in County Court or District court.

The problem is that while you may win a judgement, the piece of paper could be worthless because it is very difficult to collect money from a person with no insurance coverage. Another possibility: contact the Texas Department of Public Safety, which has the ability to suspend someone's license when they have no insurance and they caused the wreck. You may be able to use this method to try to get monthly payments from the responsible person in exchange for not suspending his license.

When DPS receives notice that there was a crash that resulted in injury, death or property damages of at least $1,000, the uninsured driver is subject to a possible drivers' license suspension. In certain circumstances, the uninsured driver may be entitled to a hearing before his/her license is suspended.

If the Texas Drivers' License is suspended, it may be reinstated if the uninsured driver has entered into an Installment Agreement to pay for any damages caused. The uninsured driver will also be required to carry SR-22 Insurance, which simply is an expensive type of insurance where the Texas Department of Public Safety is notified if the person stops paying for the insurance coverage.

When the Texas Department of Safety receives proof of a Liability Judgment (what you get from the Court if you win), it handles such matters in a very similar fashion. For more information, be sure to go to the website for Texas Department of Safety, http://www.dps.texas.gov/DriverLIcense/CrashSuspension.htm.

Can I Use My Own Insurance to Get My Car Fixed? Why would I?

Besides making a claim on the other person's insurance, you could decide instead to make a claim on your own insurance. Not everyone chooses to buy this type of insurance coverage, so be sure to check your policy or call your agent.

There are certain times when it makes sense to go through your own insurance company — for example, if the other insurance company is still investigating (perhaps there is be a dispute as to who caused the wreck). In that case, you may not want to wait to get your car fixed. And you certainly do not want your car to be stuck in some storage lot racking up fees while waiting for someone to make a determination of fault — at least, you don't want it there for long. In this situation, it is a wise decision to go ahead and pay your deductible (usually $500) and get your car fixed.

Keep in mind that you may get your deductible back if your insurance company gets the other people's insurance company to accept responsibility for the wreck. You would get a percentage of your deductible back based on the accepted percentage of fault.

For example, if the other insurance company agrees that they are 100% at-fault, then you will get 100% back of the $500 you paid. But, if the responsible insurance company only agrees that they were 75% at fault, then you would only get back $375. Also, now that you are dealing with your own insurance company, you do have a duty to cooperate with them and they may ask how the wreck happened and if you are injured. In that situation, you do have to speak with them ...however, I seriously recommend speaking with an attorney prior to making any type of call to an insurance adjuster.

If you do not have your own insurance coverage and the at-fault driver has no insurance, the only way to get the car damage paid for is to sue the other driver (and possibly the owner of the car if different). Our Justice of the Peace Courts cover legal disputes up to $10,000 and allows people to attempt to resolve their claims without an attorney. For larger amounts, there are other courts that would be proper for jurisdiction. In addition, it may be possible to have the driver's license of the other person suspended if you can show Texas DPS that the other person was at fault and that they had no automobile insurance.

IN CONCLUSION

We hope that this book has given you sound insight on how to handle a car accident claim involving you or a loved one, and if you are dealing with the aftermath of an accident, we wish you a speedy recovery.

If you have questions on any of the topics we covered in this book or would like to speak directly with an attorney about your case, please don't hesitate to contact me directly at (713) 904-1735 or visit my websites, www.attorneymcclure.com for English and www.soytuabogado.com for Spanish, for more information.

We also encourage you to learn more about us and our firm culture by visiting our social media pages, which can be found by searching "Attorney McClure" on Facebook, Twitter, or Instagram or "The Law Office of Don McClure" on LinkedIn.

Testimonials

"The Law Office of Don E. McClure were so helpful. They spent time guiding me to get on the right path in finding the lawyer my family needed. Mr. McClure took time out of his busy schedule to give me a personal recommendation of lawyer he knows well. If the office helped me without being a client of theirs, I can imagine how well they would take care their own clients. Blessings to him, his family and staff."

"Don and Edith are outstanding and clearly some of the best in the field of personal injury. After being injured in an automobile accident they assured me that I would receive the fair treatment I deserved. Throughout my case Edith was extremely knowledgeable and experienced, she walked with me step by step through the entire process. I appreciate their office for being approachable, extremely professional and pushing relentlessly throughout the process. Personally, I do not feel I could have been in better hands. Can't thank them enough. Highly recommended!"

"My family and I called the law office of Don E. McClure to help us get our mothers estate and affairs in order before her death. To say that our family was in grief is an understatement. The process of coping with a terminal cancer and then trying to find legal counsel and support would have been daunting had we not encountered this law firm who listened as we explained our needs. The compassion and caring and general understanding made our difficult situation bearable as we knew we had found wise counselors who have core legal competencies. Mr. McClure and his wife Edith walked us through the process step by step and made my mother who was already ill feel respected, loved, and certain that her wishes would be upheld. We were so pleased with Don and Edith's knowledge, organizational skills, and competency that two other families have hired him as their legal counsel. You will find the law office extremely professional, returning calls and requests in a timely manner and working overtime to assist you and your legal needs. I highly recommend this firm."

"Great service! Don and Edith explained every step of our case in detail and answered every question to help us understand the process of the case. We truly recommend them."

"Don is a family man that understands the complications of life. We don't subject ourselves into problems on purpose, but he is there to cut past the red tape and get you the best possible outcome. He is straight forward and will work with you. I've used Mr. McClure for the past decade and will continue to happily keep him in my corner. Thank you, Don."

"Don is an amazing attorney that goes out of his way and looks for the best interest of his clients. Not only is he a great attorney but has a golden heart too along with Edith. I would definitely recommend him!"

"Don and Edith are amazing! I had never used an attorney before, until I was hit in a car wreck last year on I45. I had so much trouble getting the other party's insurance to even come and take a look at my clearly totaled truck, let alone talk to me about property damage or personal injury. The second I went to Don, all the hassle and headache went away. Don and Edith did a good job of explaining the process to me and they did a phenomenal job with fighting my claim with the insurance company. They went above and beyond any expectations that I had and I will 100% use them again or recommend their services to anyone who needs an attorney!"

"Best attorney in Houston. I was very pleased with Don McClure and all his staff. Very professional and makes you feel comfortable."

"Don and Edith are very wonderful people, I have known them for a long time and they have always helped me with any legal questions that I have had. They are really people that you will have by your side in case of an accident! They do a good job and always want the best for their clients. I recommend them!"

"Don is an amazing attorney that goes out of his way and looks for the best interest of his clients. Not only is he a great attorney but has a golden heart too along with Edith. I would definitely recommend him!"

"Don helped me when I was rear ended, in October, last year. He fought for everything he could, for me. He is now, handling an separate case, and I know I'm in good hands."

"He explains the law and your options in plain English. (SE HABLA ESPAÑOL) and will help you make the best decision (short run or in the long run)."

"Professional and Great people Always trying to help you and answered all your question. GREAT STAFF OVERALL GREAT. Highly recommend attorney Don McClure. He is professional and knowledgeable with many years of legal experience and achievements."

"The Law Office of Don E. McClure was so helpful. They spent time guiding me to get on the right path in finding the lawyer my family needed. Mr. McClure took time out of his busy schedule to give me a personal recommendation of lawyer he knows well. If the office helped me without being a client of theirs, I can imagine how well they would take care their own clients. Blessings to him, his family and staff."

"Simply spectacular! I had a few concerns, however, Don quickly cleared them up. He provided me with all the information I needed without any hesitation. Extremely thankful for all his help! Would definitely recommend him time & time again."

We Would Be Happy to Help Your Loved Ones

At Attorney McClure, we treat our clients like family since many of our clients really are family or referred by family! Almost every client we have can be traced back to a family tree. Your case is not just business, it's personal. That's why every referral you send our way makes a difference. We get to help even more people and our family tree continues to grow. We are grateful for referrals and thank our clients and friends for trusting us not only to help them but help the people they care about.

If you are reading this book, you most likely receive our monthly newsletter. If not, we'd love to add you to the list - for free - since it is filled with heart-warming stories, great recipes, and tips to improve your life. Simply visit attorneymcclure.com/newsletter to start receiving and we'd be happy to send free copies to any friends or family members you feel would enjoy reading the publication.

Any time you are worried about someone in your life who was impacted by a car accident, give them the gift of free legal advice and have them call us. We will give them a complete case analysis and outline all of their options, whether or not that involves enlisting Attorney McClure to help. We can walk them through all of the tactics insurance companies use to deny the claims, give them advice on how to seek the best medical treatment, and make sure that they are getting a fair deal. We treat our firm family like real family. Every day.

Attorney McClure's VIP MEMBERSHIP PROGRAM

I invite you to take part in my free VIP Member Program. There are many benefits from the program that are briefly listed below. To review the benefits in more detail and to complete the application form, go to www.attorneymcclureVIP.com.

In about ten days after completing the application form, you should receive the VIP key ring tag to place on your key rings. I am sending this tag as a thank you for becoming a VIP Member. If you do not receive your tag within ten days, please shoot us an email to let us know.

We are also going to make sure that you will be receiving our newsletters and our calendar so that you can keep up with us. Further, please make sure you follow us on Facebook at Facebook.com - Attorney McClure by hitting "Like" and going under "Likes" and selecting "Following", "see first" to ensure you get notified of important information and contests.

Also, don't forget that VIP Membership includes:

1. A free 15 minute legal consultation (can be by scheduled phone call);
2. A free Insurance policy review;
3. Free (scheduled) notary services;
4. Automatic Entry into all Attorney McClure contests; and
5. Free return of your keys should you misplace or lose them.

We are excited that you are going to be a part of the VIP Program and we look forward to helping you reap the benefits.